TRAMPLING DOWN DEATH BY DEATH

FATHER SPYRIDON BAILEY

FaR

Also by Father Spyridon:

Journey To Mount Athos

&

The Ancient Path

To Joe

Published in 2014 by FeedARead Publishing
– financed by *The Arts Council of Great Britain.*

A CIP catalogue record for this title is available from the British Library.

Contents

Introduction

It is a cliché to say *we are all going to die*. We have heard it many times and a part of our mind knows it. But the reality of this statement is something that must shape our entire lives. Engaging with the truth of our death must become a priority if we are to live as we should.

Real death is now hidden away; it has been taken into the hands of professionals who oversee our medical care and the way our bodies die. But still most of us continue to see images of death all the time. News broadcasts repeat unimaginable numbers lost in disasters or war. Films and literature set before us the deaths of characters and we are invited to judge the events as morally just, or tragic, or even horrific. But these are not real deaths; they are fantasies that mask the reality of death. They lead us to imagine that death must be the result of some unusual event that has caught the unwary by surprise; we look on at the death of others and are reassured by the safe distance of a television screen or the knowledge that it is someone else. In fact we are all moving towards our death with every breath. The hands with which you hold this book will be lifeless. The care with which we groom our bodies, the washing and trimming, all will come to an end as others look on at us as a corpse. And what then? Does death render life absurd or pointless? Does death mean we should seek to maximise our pleasures while the going is good?

This book is a reflection on this most important of topics. I write from an Orthodox Christian perspective in the hope that readers will be awakened to the reality of their own mortality and respond by choosing to live in a way that makes sense of life and death. It is the Christian belief that the reality of death, far from stripping life of its meaning, helps us to understand the true purpose of our existence. To understand this meaning we shall consider why we die, what the Church teaches about what happens to us after biological death, how eternal life fits into our thinking, and of course how Christ's death enables us to make sense of it all. We will look at how the Church has portrayed Christ's death and resurrection and how our celebration of Pascha is an essential element to living properly in the face of death. It will also be useful to reflect on our attitudes to grief and the role of the funeral service both in terms of what we believe happens to the dead but also within the grieving process.

Ultimately I hope to communicate the core of authentic Christianity which I believe is the only means of finding true life. Therefore I base my theological reflections on those authorities recognised by the Church: The Bible, the words of the Church's services, and the writings of the

Church Fathers and saints. Within this tradition is the path that leads to eternal life, not as some future event, but in the here and now.

In the mid nineteen-nineties I served a funeral for a four year old boy who had been killed in an accident while on holiday. His parents were naturally devastated over the loss of their only child. The memory of his small white coffin being carried to the front of the church by his father still moves me. I was struck by the emotional strength of his parents who agreed never to consider the question of which of them might have been "to blame" but instead they came together in their mutual loss to grieve and support one another. But the memory that haunts me most is the confusion that was felt not just by those who knew and loved this little boy, but by many people at the time who expressed a sense of anger, including members of my own congregation. *How could God let such a thing happen to one so innocent?* Some raged, *what meaning can there be in a life cut off so tragically young?*

This book is an attempt to speak not just to those particular questions, but to so many fears and uncertainties raised by the reality of death. It is an attempt to share the hope of the Church and remind us all that we have a purpose which extends beyond the clutches of the grave. We must not fear death, for as Tertullian writes: *It is a poor thing for anyone to fear that which is inevitable.* In order to overcome our fears we need to understand what it is that frightens us and most importantly recognise that death is not the end. Our starting point will be to consider how death came into the world and the relationship between our soul and body.

Why Is There Death?

To understand why we die we have to confront a number of apparent contradictions, or rather paradoxes. All that is natural and good seems to tell us that suffering and death are evil, and certainly the Christian understanding is that God created man as body and soul and so their separation is certainly not His will for us. And yet, as we shall see in the writings of Saint John Chrysostom and particularly when we consider the issue of martyrdom, many Christians have welcomed death as an opportunity to witness to their faith or to protect the dogmas in which they believe. Furthermore we are encouraged by the logic of our worldly reasoning to recognise all suffering as something to be avoided, and that perhaps it is evil. But much that causes our suffering is not evil in itself: we cannot describe a volcano's eruption as evil even if it results in the loss of many lives. We are living in a world that is not perfect. It has been distorted, and it is this distortion that has made suffering and death a reality. The suffering we endure is a consequence of moral evil, but we can often benefit from our suffering: as Saint Basil the Great says our suffering in this life can *cut off the growth of sin*. So let us look closely at how this state of affairs came to be and what it means for us as we try to understand our mortality.

Genesis tells us that God created all things good and gave humanity free will as a being created in His image. It was our use of the free choice to disobey God that separated humanity from God's perfection. This moral evil was of such a profound nature that it affected not just man but the whole created order. Our sin disfigured the cosmos because disobedience was essentially a rejection of God and the choosing of self. If love is to be real it can not be forced, no one who is coerced into love truly loves. And if the choice to love is real, so too must be the choice not to love. This second choice is the option for evil, it is the violation we call sin.

This freedom to choose was given both to us and to the angels. Satan's pride led to himself and a third of the angelic order being cast out from Heaven: these are the demons who persist in their acts against us and God. It was Satan who first tempted humanity into rejecting God's command and who continues to attack and mislead us when given the opportunity. Death was not the punishment of an angry God of His creatures for the transgression of His laws. Rather His laws were there to protect us from the consequences of those actions which were forbidden since they lead to death. We are told in Genesis that God warned *You must not eat from the tree of knowledge of good and evil, for when you eat of it you will surely die*. This is not God threatening to kill but trying to protect us from our own foolishness. Disobedience and separation from God changed the nature of our existence; as he lost communion with the source of all light and goodness man became darkened and full of sin. But it must be made clear that while this change which is often called *the fall* disfigured the image of God within us, it did not remove it. Each of us, however sinful, retain something of the image of God without which there could be no salvation.

This disfigurement can be seen both in our soul and body. We are all inclined to the passions and must battle with greed, lust, pride and so on. But also our physical reality is corrupted too: we suffer disease and fatigue, and of course we die. This is because, as discussed in the following chapter, our physical and spiritual existence is intimately linked: we exist as both within the whole of our humanity.

The immortality with which we were created was removed from the body when we lost the fullness of communion with God. The Tree of Life described in the Garden of Eden is the symbol of the life sustained in Paradise. Once we lost our place in Paradise we also lost access to the source of that which sustains life in our bodies. God permits this consequence of our sin because in dying we are prevented from sinning eternally. In our fallen state we see disease and death and imagine them as the worst possible effect our sin has brought about, but in reality it is our loss of

Paradise that we should be more concerned with. The image of God within us maintains our distinction from the animal kingdom and it is a sign of our ability to return to that state of Paradise. If we use our free will to live like the animals then death and disease will continue to terrorise us, but if we live as those who seek a return to Paradise we may discover a freedom from the sting of death and the threat of pain. We inherit a fallen nature which is corrupted, but we are still blessed with a rational mind and an innate spiritual yearning to know and love God and be loved by Him. The greatest miseries of all stem from the denial of this inherent need, since rejection of God's love acts in direct opposition to the needs we are created with. No amount of material wealth or earthly success can replace or overcome that spiritual need which is the nature of our soul. This inherited corrupt state includes the fruit of sin which is death.

We must recognise that death violates God's purpose for us, it sits in opposition to the intended fruitfulness and communion for which we were created. The fact is that even some Christians have begun to think of death as a natural part of nature that must be accepted as part of the way things are meant to be. Reject this notion completely and see death as an affront that must be overcome. But a further paradox is, as we shall consider later, that to truly be victorious over death we must die daily to ourselves even before our biological death. Though the soul must battle with the corrupted passions within itself and the body, it does not naturally long to be separated from the body since the two will be united eternally and redeemed together. We believe that we were created for life, not for death, God is our Creator and death is the enemy. Death is really the greatest rebellion against God and only when we submit in obedience to God can we overcome this rebellion.

We can go as far to say that the choosing we speak about is really an illusion, a terrible lie. To choose God is to choose life, light and love, but rejection of this is death, destruction, and is a corruption of self which is denial of freedom. It is the law that Saint Paul speaks of working within us, the law of Christ that brings life. If we abandon this law then the law of death takes its place which is really a denial of everything that we are created to be. Let us remember the words of Psalm 118: *If I keep Your law, I find life in it and I cannot die*. This does not imply that we will be immune to biological death in this world but that the eternal life of God will already be at work within us while we exist in this mortal state. The law that Saint Paul talks about is that which would protect us from the harm we would do to ourselves, it is possible in this context to see repentance as the ultimate act of free will and our emancipation from the bondage of sin. When we repent we embrace life and reject death, when we sin we do the opposite. Saint Gregory of Nyssa writes:

Man, though set to rule, was enslaved, and he that was created free and master is overcome and enslaved by many evils.

We are prisoners to death only if we continue to give ourselves to the evils through which death entered the world. Christ came for the purpose of overcoming that final and terrible enemy of mankind, but the victory is only made ours through our participation and co-operation with His Grace.

In our funeral services the priest declares that *From dust you came and to dust you return.* The gravity of these words expresses the truth of our physical existence, that God took something of the created universe and into it breathed a spirit. This duality of our being, body and soul, sits at the heart of our natural objection to death. We understand that trees and flowers and even animals must die, but the death of a man is so much more. Even those who reject the possibility of their spiritual nature find something unacceptable and painful in human death. It is more than grief over a loved one, death itself feels like an affront to what should be. And this is because it is true, but its truth lies in more than what man is. Death is unacceptable not because we are so special in and of ourselves, but because we are loved by God. It is divine love for us that confronts our death because it is in being loved by God that we are given purpose. If our existence consisted of no more than the houses we buy, the wealth we accumulate, the family lines we contribute to or even the relationships we form, then death would render everything meaningless. But the love of God gives meaning to everything we do since God wills that we experience His love for all eternity. Immortality of the soul is a gift from God, the soul does not possess immortality as part of its essence, it is given that God may love us eternally.

When we ask why death exists we must see that no blame can be attributed to God, for God only wills love and goodness. The fear or grief that death evokes is a consequence of our own inclination to independence and self-will. If we make our will the arbiter of right and wrong then we place our soul in our own hands which cannot give eternal life. If we repent and throw ourselves on to the mercy of God we find ourselves held by the hands that first gave life and which can lead us back to Paradise.

The Significance Of The Human Body

On Mount Tabor at the Transfiguration the three Apostles, Peter, James and John saw for the first time Christ revealed as He truly is. It was not a sudden change in Christ that they witnessed, but the revelation to them of how He had always been. The opening of their eyes to the reality of Christ's true appearance (as when Moses glimpsed something of God's presence in the burning bush as it was, not because it has suddenly changed) is a sign of what the Holy Spirit is doing within all of us. The process of our theosis is the gradual change from dull matter to that which is transfigured by the uncreated light of God. We are called to be transfigured, not as ghosts, but in soul and body. It was the very flesh and even clothing of Christ that was illuminated by divine light, the material things of our physical world. As Saint Isaac the Syrian writes:

Here is the sign that you are approaching the borders of this mysterious country: when grace begins to open your eyes so that they see things in their essence.

Creation groans but also offers itself up in praise to the Creator. Our physical bodies are part of that offering through which the universe finds its meaning and purpose. It is an astounding realisation when we understand our place in the cosmic order. We actively co-operate with the divine purpose when we struggle to repent and obey God's will. The action of our transfiguration is the hymn of creation sung in worship of the giver of all good things. The control we exercise over the body's impulses and desires is therefore our choosing to participate in the restoration of creation. We are not passive onlookers to the work of redemption; God has blessed us with the responsibility to be key workers in His plan. Together we raise the world towards Heaven like incense rising in the Liturgy, the everyday choices and actions we perform can contribute to time and space becoming a cosmic act of worship: or alternatively we can follow the selfish desires of self-interest and refuse our true purpose in life.

Saint Simeon the New Theologian writes: *Having become all fire in his soul, man transmits the inner radiance gained by him also to the body, just as physical fire transmits its effect to the iron.*

The body is not an old set of clothes to be discarded at death. Many people today, including many ignorant Christians, have adopted ideas from pagan religions which teach that the soul is the only true worth of man, and that the spiritual life is about breaking free from the realm of material existence: it is seen as both natural and positive. They look to some spiritual existence where they will know the bliss of being free from a physical body which is so often the cause of pain and misery. Death is thus seen as a form of liberation. This is partly why Hindus burn the body at death, a sign that the old shell has been cast off, and can be obliterated in the flames of cremation. The Christian practice of burial is a sign of the belief that the human body is precious and plays an important part in our eternal future. The presence of the Holy Spirit within us and our attempt to live in obedience to God transforms us as whole people. While the body continues to bear the effects of sin and death in this world, we are assured that God will lift the seeds that have been planted in the ground at The Day of Judgement. We can only know true holiness when we achieve unity of body and soul: transfiguration is the union of our spiritual and material being returned to that state when God first breathed life into dust.

Resurrection includes both body and soul; we cannot read the Bible and come to any other reasonable conclusion. When the Apostles saw the risen Christ they thought He might be some kind of ghost. It was important that they understand their error and so Christ demonstrated very clearly to them that He was truly risen in His body. He took food and ate it in front of them and invited Saint Thomas to touch the wounds of crucifixion. The message preached by the early Church was that Christ was risen bodily and that at the heart of their worship was the sharing of Holy Communion which was His Body and Blood. Christians eat and drink that their bodies may physically share in the sacrament, just as the body is physically washed at baptism and anointed with oil. The sacraments are shared through the material things of the earth because it is in a new relationship to God. In the incarnation Christ not only joined Himself to the nature of our humanity but with the whole created order. Christ's incarnation makes it possible for wood and paint and every thing of the earth to be brought into worship of God. Our physical existence is dignified and the process of renewal began when Christ entered His mother's womb. But that dignity was still overshadowed by death. Christ then entered into that darkness and overcame the final enemy by *trampling down death by death*: He illuminated even the despair of the tomb with the power of His love.

It is important that we understand the role of the body in our salvation because we can then treat it and use it as it was created to be used. We must first look to the creation story in Genesis and see that God created man with a body and soul, we came into existence both spiritually and materially at the same time. Death works directly against this union of soul and body and is therefore in direct opposition to God's creative purpose. We see not just the importance of the body but also of man himself in the creation story. Unlike the rest of creation which was brought into existence by God's command or word, man was given life by God

Who breathed life into the dust of the earth. The body was formed from the earth and the soul was brought into existence simultaneously as a union of the breath of life from the mouth of God and the physical substance of creation. Man is thus given a supreme position in God's created order since he alone is made to be the meeting of the earthly and the heavenly. Christ's incarnation re-establishes this link by God Himself entering that created order to establish an eternal, unbreakable union that lifts our relationship with God to a profound new level.

This understanding of man's position in creation is made clear when God pronounces *Let us make man in Our image, after Our likeness*. The divine image within us is not to be recognised in the physical body, but in the soul, however this does not undermine the body's importance. The union of soul and body in creation demonstrates that the physical form of man must serve as a kind of companion to the soul, either bringing the soul down to the earthly desires of the dust or being lifted up to the heights of the spirit. The direction of movement that takes place is determined by which of the two, soul or body, is the predominant partner. Christ calls us to make the body a temple of the Holy Spirit, but it is easier for the soul to be dragged down into sinful passions. This is why the Church teaches its members to pursue a certain degree of aesthetic practice: by enforcing the will over the body the soul is able to rein in the harmful impulses that can result from laziness, greed or lust. It is, however, important to understand what this means. When we read of the extremes of aesthetic practice carried out by certain monastics we should not imagine that this is either something suitable for all of us or a sign that Christianity rejects the body. A monk who pays great attention to his diet and other bodily needs does so not because the body is unimportant, but quite the opposite. All of us, monks and those living in the world should see our bodies as playing a vital role in our salvation. We must seek proper medical attention when we fall ill, we should avoid recreational drugs or the excessive consumption of alcohol, because the body is the crucial companion of the soul through which we encounter God's creation and express our will. When we change the mind's capacity to perceive reality as it really is then we make ourselves vulnerable to delusion and heretical thoughts. Chemical alteration of the brain disrupts the natural purpose of our minds and interferes with our ability to make rational choices and actively seek understanding of God. Similarly a life cut short by the ravages of tobacco or a diet full of salt is a waste of God's precious gift. The limited time we each have before death should not be thrown away casually: the opportunity for repentance is God's merciful offering before the time of judgement.

The bond that exists between body and soul does not come to an end at the point of death. Christ showed that through resurrection body and soul will be raised together as a single entity once again. The body is united with that which is breathed from God: our life is a sacred blessing. The body is animated by the non-physical soul which is unlike anything that is earthly. As Saint Gregory says:

The soul is the breath of God, and while being heavenly, it endures being mixed with what is of the dust. It is a light enclosed in a cave, but still it is divine and inextinguishable.

This does not mean that the soul is itself a part of God's essence, or that the soul shares the identity of the divine nature. The soul of man is created by God; it is brought into existence just as the body owes its being to God. But what is clear is that the human soul is of a type that is not only different but is markedly superior to anything else on earth. Just as the soul is created to control and direct the body, so the body is made to accept and be governed by the soul. In order for this governance to take place the soul may at times feel that the body is in opposition to its will, that it struggles to break free from the soul's control. But only when the body is fully subjected to the dominance of the soul can the union of the two find the harmony God intended. So long as the body is free to dictate its whims over the soul there can only be conflict, disharmony and unhappiness.

This disharmony results from our choosing disobedience to God and its consequence is the wounding of both soul and body. This is not to suggest that we can always identify a direct link between the individual sin of a person and their suffering, though there are occasions when the link is clear. Since we are united in our common humanity and as part of God's created order, we share in the consequences of one another's sin, and we see the impact of our disobedience not just in the spiritual anguish that so many of us suffer, but also in the degradation of our physical being. The body therefore plays its part in our rejection of the harmony God intends for us but also suffers the results.

God has created us as part of the material world not to escape or reject it, but to recognise its role in our salvation. When we are warned to guard ourselves against the world, the flesh and the devil it is not a call to a dualistic conception of ourselves. The world is not simply the created material existence but is the attractions and snares of corruption and self-centredness. The flesh does not refer to our material being but to the unrestrained passions that will enslave us if we do not struggle to overcome our greed and lust. And of course the devil is like a circling lion who will use all of these weapons to destroy us if we are not sober and watchful. And yet what mercy God shows even to those who would deny Him. To those who would sink themselves head first into the world and the flesh, God enters the material world and speaks to them from the very substance behind which they would hide. To man who makes an idol of his own form, God draws close to him and joins Himself to his very humanity to save him from the death he has too often chosen. That the creature may rise to be grace-filled and a member of Christ's family, God enters the limits of His creatures' form and submits Himself in humility and lowliness.

We should therefore understand biological death as a temporary interruption of God's plan for us. It temporarily prevents the human person from fully expressing the life that God has given by denying the soul its full expression through the body. It does not, however, completely separate the soul from the body; it can not dismantle the union that God created at the very moment of the creation of man. We are one being, body and soul, and the distress of death is more than psychological loss or emotional bereavement. It is the moment we are confronted with the reality and horror of what our sin has done. Death is an outrage, and without faith in Christ's resurrection it makes a mockery of every human hope or sense of nobility. But as we shall see, the funeral service does not express devastation or hopelessness, it celebrates victory.

Immortality Of The Soul

The death of someone we love or the realisation that we ourselves are going to die raises many important questions in our mind. We want to know if we will still be conscious or if we enter some kind of sleep when our bodies stop functioning. We wonder if our loved ones retain their identity, whether the spirit goes straight to Heaven or must wait in some in-between state. We may ask whether the dead have any awareness of us who remain on earth and whether they retain an interest in our lives. The Christian faith has answers to these questions but there is confusion amongst many people since they are unaware of what the Church has always believed. This confusion is only made worse by the heretical teachings of different sects which have appeared in the last few centuries and which peddle their beliefs in the name of Christianity. Just because a group calls itself the "Church" does not mean it has anything to do with the life and teachings of Christ or His Apostles. We must guard ourselves against these false doctrines because what we believe happens to us after death has a profound effect on what we do in our lives. This chapter will therefore deal with some of the heresies that exist and then present the authentic teaching of Christianity.

The first idea we must dismiss is what has often been called "conditional immortality" or "soul-sleep". This is the belief that when the body dies the soul enters a kind of suspended animation until the day of universal resurrection. It is argued that ideas about the soul continuing on after death owe their origin to Greek philosophers such as Plato rathcr than Christ or the Old Testament. Certainly there are groups such as the Malabar in the West Indies who have held this heretical belief for some time, but as we shall see, it does not conform to the belief and practice of the undivided Church.

Protestant reformer Martin Luther rejected the idea of the immortality of the soul because he believed it to be a creation of the Roman Catholic Church. Observing the abuses of indulgences which were sold to relieve the sufferings of those in purgatory (see later chapter) he went too far in his reaction and rejected the very idea that the soul could exist outside of the body.

A couple of decades after Luther was John Calvin who, though he recognised Luther's error, calling those who believed in "soul-sleep" as *babblers, madmen and dreamers*, went on to make new errors of his own. He taught that Christ went immediately to Heaven at His death because he saw the body as a "prison" from which Christ had been released. He developed a further heresy known as double-predestination which maintains that God pre-ordained who would be saved and who would be rejected: thus reducing the role of our free will within our spiritual lives to nothing more than an illusion.

The key verses for those who believe in soul-sleep are when Saint Paul refers to those who *sleep in Jesus* in his first letter to the Thessalonians (Ch. 413-18). In fact Saint Paul is talking about the perspective of those who have not yet died when the general resurrection occurs. Taking the verse out of context removes it from the point he is conveying about Christians having hope as opposed to the sorrow of those who do not believe.

These false teachings spread through out the Protestant world. For example John Wycliffe and William Tyndale espoused soul-sleep and the Church of England nearly fell victim to its infection. The Thirty-nine Articles that form the basis of Anglican theology originally consisted of Forty-two Articles under Edward VI. In the reign of Elizabeth I reference to the sleep of souls was removed as it was recognised to be inconsistent with both the Bible and Christian practice.

At the heart of the problem for those who would like to imagine that the soul enters a state of slumber at biological death is the issue of hell and eternal suffering: this is treated at length in a later chapter. But the mistake these Protestant thinkers made was in their understanding of God's judgement. The idea of anyone living in an eternal state outside of Paradise painted God in their minds as unloving and far worse than any evil dictator who had found power amongst the human race. To satisfy themselves they claim that the death of the unsaved means they will *return to the dust from which they came*: of course, only man's physical form was taken from the earth, the soul came into existence from the breath of God, but still they argue for annihilation of the soul. From this perspective the dangers of hell become no more than a rod with which to beat the ignorant in order to keep them in line, but when we look at the words of Jesus we gain a very different perspective.

The Church's belief in the immortality of the human soul forms the basis of her life and worship. We believe that those we love continue on after the body's death. It was unthinkable for the Early Church to imagine the great heroes of the faith such as the Apostles and the many martyrs were anywhere but in the loving embrace of God. But before we look at this practice and what this means in terms of where we go after death let us first consider a few of the references in the Bible to the continuation of the soul after death.

The words of Ecclesiastes assure us that at death: *Then shall the dust return to the earth as it was and the spirit shall return to God who gave it.* (Eccl. 12[7]) The reality of immortality is found through out the Old Testament, we read Moses describing God as taking Enoch without undergoing death (Genesis

5^{24}) and we read at the deaths of Abraham, Moses and Aaron that they were *gathered to their people*.

In Hebrews $12^{22\text{-}24}$ we read:

You have come to Mount Zion and to the city of the living God, the heavenly Jerusalem, to an innumerable company of angels, to the general assembly and Church of the first-born who are registered in Heaven, to God the judge of all, to the spirits of just men made perfect.

Here we see reference to the Church in Heaven which has passed beyond death. The Early Church understood this to mean that these souls were alive with Christ; they had retained their identity and consciousness while waiting for the final judgement to come.

At His crucifixion Christ promised the thief who was dying on the cross beside Him that that very day he would be in Paradise (Luke 23^{43}). It was not the promise of Paradise at the end of a long sleep, but the guarantee of something immediate and near. Jesus clearly believed that both His and the soul of the man on the cross beside Him were going to live on beyond the death that their bodies were being subjected to.

Again in Luke $20^{37\text{-}38}$ Jesus says:

But even Moses showed in the burning bush passage that the dead are raised...For He is not the God of the dead but of the living, for all live to him.

At the Transfiguration (Matthew $17^{1\text{-}9}$ we see Moses and Elijah appearing with Christ. There is no doubt in the Apostles' minds that this is anything but the real presence of those who live beyond the visible realm of life. They did not imagine they were seeing an illusion or some kind of projected memory of those who had lived: they understood clearly that Moses and Elijah were appearing before them because their life continued with God.

An important reference is Hebrews 12[1] when Saint Paul refers to the Christians who have died as a great cloud of witnesses. While the issue of the saints and the Church on earth's relation to the "Church Victorious" is dealt with in a later chapter, we should note here that someone can not be a witness if they are asleep. To witness implies consciousness, it implies life and identity, it points to the life of the soul beyond the body.

When we read the account of the end of this world in the Book of Revelation we discover Saint John describing the activities of the saints in Heaven. He portrays them worshipping before the throne of God and casting their crowns to the King of Glory. Saint John describes all of this before what is called the Great Tribulation: it is the activity of the saints now, while we live in time on earth. Such activity cannot be attributed to one who sleeps, it is contradictory to attribute the lifeless state of soul-sleep to the dead and at the same time acknowledge the life-filled activity of worship and praise which is offered to God by them. Seventh Day Adventists and other Protestants are thus faced with abandoning their heresy or else denying the words of Holy Scripture.

This rather technical issue is important because it affects deeply the way we think about our loved ones when they die. To know that they have not ceased to exist or that their consciousness has been obliterated means that the bond of love between us has not come to an end. The Christian faith assures us that the Church exists both in Heaven and on earth. The support we offer one another through prayer continues to maintain this bond, and as shall be shown in our next chapter, prayer to the saints is a powerful manifestation of our belief in the immortality of the soul.

Atheism contends that what is called the soul is really no more than an expression of what exists within the physical form of a person. Even amongst some modern philosophers there exists the belief that the mind also is no more than a side-product of our material existence, they liken it to "the stench from a dirty pool". Self-consciousness is therefore no more than an illusion of something which does not really exist. The "self" is reduced to an effect of electrical impulses within the brain which have no ultimate purpose or value beyond survival and procreation. This low view of man is opposed by the Christian faith. Christ's incarnation declares us to be of supreme value to God, and that every individual human being is infinitely more valuable than all of the world's works of art or the greatest mountain with which the earth is adorned.

The human soul is a mystery; there is no absolute explanation within scripture or dogma which fully accounts for how we come into existence beyond the metaphorical language of Genesis. The Church rejects any notion that our souls pre-exist our physical life, we do not believe that before coming to earth we each experience an existence in another realm of spirit. The Genesis account certainly makes clear God's relationship to our coming into existence, but while the account of the creation of the first man and woman are one thing, we do not have any dogmatic account of the role of the souls of parents in the creation of their children's souls. Certainly some of the Church Fathers (such as Tertullian and Gregory the Theologian) taught that just as the physical form of a person comes into existence from the sexual union of his parents, so too the mother and father's souls contribute to the creation of their child's spiritual existence. It would be unwise to speculate too much on this issue, only to say that whatever the creative process that results in the soul, the Church absolutely maintains belief in its existence. When we consider the qualities of our loved ones which so clearly distinguish them from the animal kingdom, their moral courage, awareness of beauty, the ability to admire art and music, then it is unthinkable to imagine that they have simply ceased to exist. All those good things that we see in man are the expression of God's image within us. Even beyond the assurance of Holy Scripture, the witness of the saints or teaching of the Church at the prompting of the Holy Spirit, some part of us knows intuitively that there is more to man than chemistry and electrical impulses. There has been some disagreement over whether the soul is immortal by nature, being brought into existence with this quality, or whether it is made immortal by God's Grace Who alone is immortal in His essence: the fact is both positions see the soul's immortality as ultimately being a gift from God. To believe in a loving God is to believe that He will not allow us to fall beyond His love and living presence. The bond that exists between man and God is eternal, our faith insists in a hope that reaches beyond the grave to the One Who is not contained by time and the limits of this universe. Believing that we live on after physical death should take from us the fear of death but should also convince us of the seriousness with which we need to view our eternal condition. The meaning of our life is found in our response to that first moment of creation when God's breath filled the inanimate dust: we are called to strive towards the source of the image within us, find union with Him so that we may glorify the artist Who created us by being all that we were given the potential to be. We are made to reach up to the majesty of God, becoming gods by Grace and eternally moving towards His perfection.

The Communion of Saints

From the beginning of the Church's existence the belief in the immortality of the soul was expressed through its worship and prayer. If anyone is in doubt about the Church's belief in the immortality of the soul he need look no further than the prayers and services that make up her spiritual life. The faith of the Church proclaims that she is truly one in Christ in Whom and through Whom death has been transcended. Biological death does not create any spiritual separation between the living and the dead: all members of the Church both on earth and in Heaven continue to be living parts of Christ's body. The love that is shared on earth does not end when the physical life of a person ends. As we shall see, this is a very different reality to the one proclaimed by spiritualists.

When someone dies we can do three things: pray for them, ask them for their prayers, or simply forget them in our prayers. From the very earliest records of Christian activity we know that Christians prayed for their dead. Saint Paulinus, one of the generation of martyrs immediately after the New Testament period, was not only prayed for, but his tomb stone was used as an altar on which the gathered community of Christians celebrated the Eucharist. The nearness to his physical remains expressed their belief that his body and soul were still mysteriously linked so that to be near his grave brought them closer to a loved one they believed to be with God. As we have noted, it was unimaginable to the Church that the first heroes of the faith, The Apostles, the Theotokos, the many martyrs, could be any where but with God in Heaven. Christ overcame death and those joined to Him in life continue to be with Him after death.

The main purpose of prayer for the dead is to continue to ask God to forgive their sins. Even the most righteous of men have sinned, for we know that only Christ lived without sin. In his letters to the new churches, Saint Paul asked for their prayers because he understood the power of prayer: God has chosen to hear us and make our prayer powerful. But when the Church is convinced of the holiness of someone, that they have lived a life of particular sanctity, and especially if that sanctity is accompanied by their willingness to shed their blood for Christ or having performed miracles during their life on earth or after their biological death, then the Church is able to pray with confidence to them asking them to join their prayers with us on earth. We venerate these holy people because they have grown in Christ's image and through them we glorify God. Just as they expressed their love for their brothers and sisters in the Church on earth, so we believe they continue to do so before the throne of God in Heaven. Many Protestants are keen on the term *fellowship*, but they should know that the Church enjoys fellowship here and with the saints in Heaven.

Their prayers are now more powerful because we believe that being so near to the throne of God, near to god Himself (as the Book of Revelation tells us they are) then His divine presence cannot but purify them and make them more holy. In Heaven they retain their consciousness and identity and remain fully aware of the events and people on earth. They are actively involved with the struggles and temptations of their brother and sisters and answer our prayers when we ask for their help. Christ's parable of the rich man and Lazarus (Luke Chapter 16) shows us how Abraham was able to hear the cries of the rich man even from Hades. Their understanding and love can only be intensified in Heaven; when we pray we should remember the invisible multitude that stands with us, both angelic and saintly, and see our time here on earth in the perspective of the continuation of life with Christ.

Christian history is full of examples where saints who have died have been seen by members of the Church on earth. When Saint Ignatius (Bishop of Antioch) was martyred in the jaws of lions (in around AD 110), his flock returned home in tears and grief. But they told of how that night they had seen the saint praying for them and even embracing some of them. Their hearts were filled with hope and courage through this glimpse of his heavenly presence, and many of them went on to give their own lives for Christ with the assurance that the brutality that ended their life here could not prevent them from living on.

In more recent times Saint Nektarios, Bishop of Pentapolis in Egypt (d.1920) has appeared to many people in both dreams and visions. His presence has been accompanied by the giving of spiritual counsel and miraculous healing of the sick. He speaks to encourage and support those in need, reassuring them of God's love and mercy.

Alongside these events are also the everyday experiences of all Orthodox Christians. Few of us have never walked into a church and sensed the presence of the saints depicted in the icons. The images draw us closer to them in Heaven, like windows to the spiritual reality. Similarly being close to relics can frequently assure us of their living reality. Our homes too are adorned with icons and it is a familiar experience to us to be reassured when we pray that they are with us. In my own life I have also been blessed to sense certain saints in a tangible and surprising way. The first took place when I was on Mount Athos. I had foolishly left the path to find a short cut when walking between monasteries. As exhaustion took over I began to wonder if I was going to succumb to the heat and tiredness. As I prayed for help to the Theotokos I had a powerful sense of her with me, strengthening me and assuring me. Her presence was very different to that sense of God's presence; she had a presence of sweetness and gentleness, the presence of a loving mother. I had not expected such an experience, it lifted all fear from me and I understood a little of why Mount Athos is dedicated to her.

While visiting Corfu to visit the incorrupt body of Saint Spyridon I stood with the crowd of pilgrims for about an hour waiting for my turn to kiss his feet. During that time I was struck by how near he was, how close to us was his loving and living presence. Again it caught me by surprise, I wasn't feeling particularly "spiritual" or even prayerful, but out of the blue came the reality of what had brought me and many others from our respective nations. His presence was almost more real than that of the strangers around me, and as he made himself known to me tears flowed down my cheeks. As I finally approached his body I understood with my head and heart that here was a man so utterly filled and transformed by God's spirit that he had been permitted to make his love known to us here on earth. At such a moment the question of whether there is life beyond death is answered absolutely, it is like asking someone if the sky exists or if night follows day.

To some, such accounts will be as yet beyond their belief, because the reality of that unseen world is no more than an idea or concept. Others will hear of these events and know their truth because their hearts are already filled with the reality of Heaven, knowing that God has permitted such things to strengthen and uplift the faithful. Others will shy away from such stories because they fear that they sound too much like spiritualism. Therefore it is worth making clear how the things believed in and experienced by the Church have nothing to do with those occult practices forbidden by God.

In Leviticus (Chapters 19 and 20) and in 1 Samuel (Chapter 28) God's servants are forbidden from attempting to communicate with the dead by summoning spirits or seeking the help of mediums. After the terrible loss of life during the First World War many people in Britain felt unable to cope with their bereavement and in their grief tried to speak to their dead at séances and spiritualist meetings. Perhaps the churches should look to themselves to partly explain why these people felt they weren't being given the answers they needed. Clergymen still affected by liberal theologies and rationalist philosophies too often shunned the simple truths of the Church, they themselves were unclear about the true faith of Christianity, and offered only weak substitutes that could never satisfy the needs of grieving souls.

But ancient Christianity does not summon up the dead. We believe that all are alive in Christ and our union in love and prayer continues. The terrible reality for those who turn to mediums is that many are simply being deceived by charlatans, while others fall prey to demonic forces which masquerade as the souls of family members in order to lead them away from God. As Saint John Chrysostom reminds us:

It is not possible for a soul, once separated from its body, to wander here any more. For the souls of the righteous are in the hands of God... and the souls also of sinners are straight away led away hence... and it cannot be that a soul, when it has gone out of the body may wander here.

Clearly Saint John is talking about the majority of ordinary souls and not those who are so filled with God's Grace and holiness that their prayer in Heaven has an exceptional effect, even to the point of God permitting us to be aware of them so that we may seek their intercession. There is no legalistic pronouncement of what God can and cannot do: only strict guidelines to protect us from evil.

The question may then be asked, *If they are in heaven why do our loved ones need our prayers? And if they are not, what good will our prayers be to them?* In order to understand this we must first emphasise that what happens to us after death is determined by what we have done before death. If we die with a repentant heart full of hope in Christ's mercy then our hope will not be in vain. But union with Christ and entry into Heaven does not instantly make us perfect. Just as we are engaged in the process of purification here on earth, sanctification, so this process continues after death. When we pray for one another's transformation here, so too we can pray that those who have died will draw closer to God and know more of Him. Christianity has never taught that someone who utterly rejected God can be saved from hell by the prayer of others, but as Saint John Damascene says:

For those dead who are unworthy of salvation, God moves none to pray for them: neither parents, nor wife, nor husband, nor relatives, nor friends.

And again he adds:

Miserable are those among the dead for whom none of the living prays.

Many saints have taught that prayer for the dead is a comfort to the dead; we are not left helpless or unable to do anything worthwhile when our loved ones die. In grief there is so often a painful longing to express our love in a way that does not feel empty or meaningless. Imagining that they have been cut off from us completely can create this false sense of hopelessness. But the good news is that through the heat of our grief we can turn that rush of feeling into something positive. They are not lost to us and we can comfort them in death just as the saints can pray for us.

In Roman Catholicism there exists a strict and rather legalistic understanding of who or what a saint is. To be canonised a Roman Catholic saint must undergo various procedures that require official verification at numerous stages. This is not how the Church has conducted its business. When someone who is known to have lived a holy life dies, it has always been natural for those who knew of their holiness to seek their prayers. This instant or local recognition of sainthood can be extended to our loved ones. Bishop Kallistos Ware says that it is perfectly acceptable and good for an orphaned child to seek the prayers of his devout parents. To maintain the contact with our loved ones through prayer is God's will. We are not praying to them to do anything in their own power or through their own might, only to join us and surround us in prayer to God. When Saint Nektarios heals the sick, he does so through God's power, through God's healing mercy. Once the saints' prayers begin to be recognised as powerful and word of their miracles spread, it is only to be expected that people from other towns or even other nations will seek their intercession. And once a saint's holiness has become established and accepted by the Church at large the Orthodox would recognise that person as unquestionably being in Heaven and worthy of veneration.

When Saint Helen went in search of the cross in Jerusalem she was faced with uncertainty about what she had found. She trusted that it was God's will for this holy object to be recovered, but in finding the cross she needed a way of verifying its authenticity. The question was answered when a man who had recently died was placed in contact with the wood and he was brought back to life. The miracle confirmed that this was the cross on which Christ had faced death and overcome it through His resurrection. The event is a good illustration of how physical objects can be blessed with God's Grace and so enable miracles to occur. No one imagined the wood of the cross itself performed the miracle, it was the holiness given to it by Christ's death. Just as water can be blessed and so used to bless other things, material objects can retain and impart God's Grace. The Church is familiar with this in its use of icons (see later chapter) but also in its use of relics.

Just as in the way the Christians who knew Saint Paulinus drew close to his physical remains to be nearer to is soul in Heaven, so the Church has always maintained the link between physical remains and the saints' spiritual existence. A biblical example would be the cloak of Saint Peter which was used to raise the dead to life. The bond between the soul and the body is eternal: we shall be raised at the Day of Resurrection as God reunites our material and spiritual existence. God's creative impulse united us as body and soul, and so the bones of saints maintain their link with the saint alive with God. Every Orthodox altar has sealed within it relics of saints so that the worship of the Church is gathered before God alongside the praise of the saints in Heaven. At the Divine Liturgy the priest and people pray with angels and with their loved ones before God's throne. In fact, just as prayer can strengthen the bond between the members of the Church on earth, so too can it strengthen our unity with the heavenly Church. Prayer both expresses and acts on our love. It is motivated by love but deepens it too. The love we feel for our friends and family who have died does not have to be put away because of the pain it might bring, it should be allowed to fill us with prayer for them. It is a part of our earthly ministry to pray for one another and it continues to be part of the Church in Heaven's to pray for us.

When Jesus faced crucifixion he prayed for His followers. Saint John's Gospel recounts His words:

All Mine are Yours and Yours are Mine...the glory You gave to me I have given to them, that they may be one even as We are One.

Christ prays that we should be one even as He and the Father are one: united in complete and eternal love. We are unified when we love one another because God is love, Three Persons united in perfect, infinite love. Our union is as eternal as the union of the Holy Trinity (though not pre-existent). When we venerate the saints, seek their prayers and pray for our loved ones, this eternal love engulfs us. The healing, life-giving power of God's love reaches beyond the grave and so let none of us fear that we have lost those we cherish.

This faith finds its expression not just in the private prayers of our homes, but week by week in our parish churches. In the words of the Divine Liturgy we are reminded again and again of the communion we share with the saints. We pray with

all those who have gone before us to their rest: patriarchs, prophets, apostles, preachers, evangelists, martyrs, confessors, ascetics, and every righteous spirit made perfect in faith.

The Divine Liturgy is the place where we step out of earthly time and enter the deepest moment of heavenly presence. The offering of bread and wine that they may become Christ's Body and Blood for us is the miraculous changing of simple things of the earth to the presence of the Creator of all. In this sublime event earth and Heaven are at their closest, prayers unite us with the saints and our loved ones in a sublimely intimate way. Loved ones that may have slipped from our minds at times due to the concerns of our earthly lives are now closer to us than at any other time: and we are assured that even when we forget them their love and concern for us never ceases.

Christ's Death

To walk into a Roman Catholic church is usually to be confronted with the image of a crucifix. The death and resurrection of Christ stands at the very centre of the Christian faith. But western art has emphasised the physical suffering of Christ, the human anguish, the blood and sweat: it is a very human perspective. This is because western art reflects a different understanding of our Lord's death to the belief of the Church. When we view an Orthodox icon of the Crucifixion we are not filled with horror. This is not to suggest that the Orthodox do not have a place for the terrible suffering that Christ endured for us, only that we do not emphasise it in the way western thought has done.

This difference in artistic representation is more than aesthetic sensitivity; it reflects the very real differences in the theologies of the cross. In order to understand death we must have a true grasp of why Christ died. This chapter will present the ancient teaching of the Church as it has existed from the time of Christ and the Apostles, and then we will look carefully at some of the heretical ideas that have developed so that we can be absolutely clear how we should hold on to the meaning of the cross in our lives.

The Apostles make it clear in their writings that we must understand salvation in two ways: that which pertains to the whole of humanity and that which is specific to each of us personally. It is vital that we understand this difference because otherwise we can misinterpret their teaching and come to false conclusions. The salvation of humanity has been accomplished. When we read in the New Testament of salvation as something fulfilled it is this general form which Christ achieved through His death and resurrection. But they also speak of an individual, personal salvation which each of us must actively participate in. The whole debate about salvation by works or faith is a false one which fails to make the distinction between this general and specific salvation. It is through God's Grace alone that humanity has been rescued from death, but each of us must actively work to make that salvation something we experience. The old question "Are you saved?" really is dangerous, because it relies on a notion that our individual salvation can be something that is done and dusted, and that we can live with the assurance of a job completed. This is in direct contradiction with the teaching of the Apostles: Saint Paul warns us about the race we are running and that as athletes must maintain their effort to the very end we must maintain our spiritual struggle lest we fall away and do not make the finish line. For each of us personally, salvation is a process which we are called by God to enter. It is the acquisition of eternal life that is both a free gift from God for which we must work to receive. To join ourselves to He Who is perfect we must cast off that which is evil within us. The path of repentance is simple but hard to follow: it requires vigilance and faith; it is the spiritual warfare in which we are Christ's soldiers.

We should see Christ's actions as opening the doorway to Paradise for us, but if we sit back and do not move towards the door we will never go through it. And what is this door, we might ask, it is none other than Christ Himself. Our struggle unites us to Christ; it is His life which begins to grow in us. The Holy Spirit enters us at our chrismation and if we co-operate then we are forever being drawn closer to God.

Let us look more closely at these two parts of our salvation, beginning with the general form. The salvation of mankind was not simply accomplished by Christ's crucifixion, it was the whole incarnation that makes our salvation possible. We must not focus only on the cross to understand how God has made the salvation of humanity possible. His death was the ultimate act of love and self-sacrifice, but by uniting Himself with our humanity God has changed us. The coming of the Holy Spirit at Pentecost is made possible by Christ's uniting of humanity with God. He unites Himself with the living and the dead. We believe that when he died on the cross He descended into Hades to reach those who had lived and died before His incarnation. It is interesting to note that just as John the Baptist, the Forerunner, went before Christ in the world to prepare the way of His coming, so too Saint John was beheaded before Christ's death: the Forerunner went ahead of Him to announce even to the dead that Christ was coming to redeem them. God's mercy extends beyond time and space, there is no one forgotten or abandoned by God. Those of us who mourn should hold on to this fact: our loved ones are alive to God.

This raising from Hades of the souls of the dead is a sign that Christ has overcome the curse placed on humanity in Genesis. Adam and Eve were cast out for their sin and death was the fruit of their actions both for them and all generations after them. Similarly the penalties of the Law of Moses are overcome. Christ has brought life to replace the curse of death; He has put right what man had done wrong. This is the general salvation which is offered to all men. Let us now see how it is possible for us to enter this new form of life.

Saint Paul calls his listeners to be *reconciled* to God (2 Corinthians 5^{20}). The Church baptises those who would be followers of Christ because the general salvation is made personal in the resurrection of Christ and us. Reconciliation has often been translated in terms of ransom, and while this has its place in our understanding, we must not interpret our salvation along the narrow lines that such a concept might suggest. If we think of Christ paying a ransom for us then we must inevitably ask to whom the ransom was paid. If someone is held captive, the ransom is paid to the hostage-taker to set them free. The idea that the all-powerful God should have to offer His only-begotten Son as a payment to Satan is ridiculous. The devil is a created being, a fallen angel; he has no capacity to force God into such a position.

The issue results from the translation of the original Greek. In the New Testament there are two words used which we translate as ransom but which have different meanings. The first is *lytro-o* which is more akin to the idea of paying a ransom and this is the one used when speaking of the general salvation of mankind. But when we look at how this word is used by the Apostles we see it in the context of ransoming us from debt or slavery, it is used to express the belief that Christ liberated us from the curses mentioned earlier, but also from slavery to evil.

The other Greek word translated in English as ransom is *agorazo* which refers to the action of purchasing for oneself: It is this word we see used in the context of the salvation of the individual (for example in 1Corinthians7[23]). When we read the New Testament we discover that the action of purchasing is not done by us but by Christ Who is shown buying us. We become the possession of Christ through obedience, when we make ourselves slaves to Him. And yet Christ goes beyond this relationship of master and slave. Time and again he calls us to be children of God, to be His brothers and sisters. Our personal relationship with Christ is fundamental to our salvation.

The western emphasis on Christ's suffering as a means of atonement has skewed its understanding of the human body and its relation to suffering. The phrase "penal substitution" is used amongst Protestants to describe how Christ's physical suffering was a fulfilment of a judicial requirement for punishment. Christ suffers these terrible pains so that we might be released from them. It assumes that if Christ had not endured the whip and nails we would have been punished by God in a way that involved such suffering. The idea is that Christ died to satisfy God's wrath, to take from us His terrible retribution. It paints a picture of a vengeful God Who must be satisfied in some way. Of course the Protestant argument is that it really shows His love because he satisfies His anger by punishing his own Son. An initial difficulty here is that it limits what God can do. God is portrayed as having to kill Jesus on the cross as this notion of justice must be fulfilled regardless of how much He wants to show mercy. In a sense God's hands are tied by His own justice: a victim must be offered one way or another. Anselm of Canterbury (1033 – 1109) created what was known as the *satisfaction theory* which showed God as demanding satisfaction of his righteous anger. This is why western art depicts

Christ on the cross in all His broken tragedy. Orthodoxy, however, maintains His divinity even in death, so that it is clear He dies to raise mankind, to overcome death, not to appease an angry judge. Christ conquers death; He is not the victim of so many Roman Catholic crucifixes. He remains the High Priest and King even in the face of physical persecution, it is a reality only seen through the eyes of faith.

There is a further problem with the Protestant idea and that is how the death of Christ actually achieves a satisfaction of God's judgement. The Church certainly believes that Christ identified with us, He became one of us so that He could take our suffering onto Himself. He enters into the reality of our humanity at its worse: not as a Lord in a castle but as one rejected, reviled and murdered. He identifies with us at our weakest and most vulnerable state; he unites Himself with us as we experience the full ramifications of what our sin has made of the world.

In the writings of the Church Fathers we find the Church's beliefs about Christ's death made clear. Justin Martyr proclaims that Christ *was not cursed by the law*. The thrust of his writing is that Christ did not bear the curse placed on Adam in any legalistic sense. Justin Martyr helps us to see the death of Christ as healing us rather than appeasement of God. Salvation and healing are parts of the same process. It is the healing of our soul through its cleansing of the wounds of sin that is at the same time the process of our salvation. When we look at the cross we are not to see the symbol of an angry God or the instrument of Christ's torture. We must rejoice in the tool of our restoration, the means of our healing where Christ united the full power and majesty of God with the broken reality of our weakness. Of course Christ did this through great personal cost, and we should remain grateful for His willingness to endure death in this way, but we must always be looking through the prism of the resurrection which reveals the true light hidden to the human eye.

Eusebius of Caesarea (the fourth century writer of Constantine's biography) writes:

How can He make our sins His own, and be said to bear our iniquities? He takes into Himself the labours of the suffering members, and makes our sickness His, and suffers all our woes and labours by the laws of love.

When the pain and grief of this world makes life difficult, we are assured of a God of infinite love and compassion Who understands our suffering from the inside. We turn to Him not just because in His infinite understanding He is able to empathise with our condition, but because we know he has suffered death as a human being like us. When we mourn our loved ones let us remember that Christ's body also lay dead in the tomb, that the darkness surrounded Mary's Child just like our dead. His love is so great that He has willingly entered into the reality of all that we would often rather run away from and not just experienced it, but overcome the greatest of all our enemies: death. Eusebius teaches that Christ did not bear our curse in some legalistic penalty, but in love carries both the burdens we suffer and the evil we commit. Christ's healing is of our wounds and of the wounds we create in others. It is not to appease an angry father but to overcome the evil we commit by allowing us to commit evil against Him. He unites Himself with us even as we crucify Him, His love and power overcoming every evil that would keep us from God. It is Satan's tyranny of pain and death that Christ frees us from: the ransom in this sense is paid to annul the dominion of death and should not be mistaken as an offering to Satan.

These two themes of healing and the destruction of death are found throughout the New Testament and in the Church Fathers who interpreted them. It is a cleansing from sin, not a serving of a sentence. Two further key figures whose writings will help us to clarify our understanding are Athanasius and Gregory of Nazianzus.

Saint Athanasius, writing in the fourth century, was influenced by the thinking of Irenaeus of Lyons before him. The starting point for Athanasius is that death is the consequence of corruption which results from sin. Protestant writers have interpreted this as meaning that death is "the penalty for sin" but this is not how Athanasius saw it. In keeping with the mind of the Early Church Athanasius does not think of corruption in judicial terms, but as a natural and inevitable consequence of our sin. Protestant thinking identifies our sin as a breaking of law, a transgression. Athanasius however, acknowledges that there is a breaking of law when we sin, but that the real issue is the injury it causes us. It points to the fundamental question of why God would give laws at all. If we imagine it is because God wants to maintain His tight control for the sake of being in charge, then perhaps we could accept the Protestant viewpoint. But most of us would reject such a notion. God gives laws to protect us, to set the boundaries of how we should conduct our lives. The laws of God are given to protect and guide us, and so any transgression does not result in a furious judge hunting us down for stepping over the line, but in sickness of soul.

The real danger of sin is that it breaks our communion with God since it is an act of turning away from His perfection and goodness. Since God is the source of life, we are turning from life to death. Had sin been no more than the breaking of laws, Athanasius makes clear that our seeking of forgiveness would be enough: when we repent surely God would be able to forgive us. We see Christ forgiving people's sins in the New Testament; it does not rely on His death in order for

God to be willing to forgive. But sin affects us far more deeply than in terms of guilt or legal transgression. The very image of God within us has been defaced; we have wounded ourselves spiritually and need healing. The image of God must be restored which requires more than a seeking of and a giving of forgiveness. Acquittal from a judge might take from us the need to be punished, but it does not restore us to the sinless state that God created us in. The Church Fathers therefore see the Crucifixion of Christ in what could be described as medical terms rather than legal concepts. Saint John Chrysostom proclaimed the Church as a place of healing rather than judgement.

Athanasius represents this mystery as being a recreation of our being, following the New Testament idea of us being new creatures born again through the womb of the font. Christ became human that the image of God would be recreated within humanity. The healing or restoration of what had been defaced by sin is achieved not just in a single event, even one as important as the crucifixion, but through the whole incarnation as was mentioned previously. Athanasius writes:

In order to effect this re-creation, however, He had to first do away with death and corruption. Therefore he assumed a human body, in order that in it death might "once and for all be destroyed", and that men might be renewed according to the image.

It is only fair to ask the same question as was asked of the Protestant beliefs: how can Christ's death have brought this about? The Fathers explain this in terms of Christ's two natures: that He is both man and God. Since He is a man He is able to die, but being God he is able to raise Himself from the dead. God goes down into the tomb of death in Him, but humanity is raised from the dead in Him too. Only One Who is both God and man can achieve this, since if He was God alone His resurrection, though miraculous, would have no effect on us (and in fact would be impossible since He would not have been able to die in the first place). Athanasius writes

The death of all was consummated in the Lord's body, yet because the Word was in it, death and corruption were in the same act utterly abolished.

Christ's death brings about the deepest possible change in us. It is a universal change to the reality of being human but at the same time each of us must use our free will to make that change personal to us. All notions of retribution and God's anger at law breakers are cast aside. The Church's understanding of Christ's death as being a means of healing is rooted in a God of love and compassion and nothing more. The simple motive of love is not tarnished with legalistic heresies; God has overthrown the law of death and sin.

Gregory of Nazianzus reminds us that Christ *became sin itself* in order to achieve the destruction of the curse that we have brought upon ourselves. Christ does not in any way fulfil the curse; He removes from us all condemnation. But we need to be careful in the way we interpret this. The Church Fathers did see humanity as guilty, we have broken God's laws and we have been disobedient. But Christ's incarnation, death and resurrection have replaced retributive justice with the economy of Grace. God has restored life, He has sanctified us, renewed us, as an act of His love for us.

Even Augustine of Hippo who had such a huge impact on the thinking of both Roman Catholics and Protestants can be seen to confirm this earlier position. He writes:

Death was condemned that its reign might cease and cursed that it might be destroyed. By Christ's taking our sin in this sense, its condemnation is our deliverance.

Augustine recognised that Christ cancelled our guilt. He continues:

Death found nothing in Him to punish, so the devil might be overcome and conquered not by power and violence but by truth and justice.

For Augustine it is Christ's innocence that is emphasised, the injustice of His death exhausts the punishment, it makes it null and void. We do not find here the Protestant understanding of appeasement to an angry God. So even those

Christians who talk about God's righteous anger must understand that the cross does not satisfy this impulse, instead it removes from us anything that could cause such anger (but this remains an extremely anthropomorphic view of God which fails to grasp the true motive of love).

We see in the difference between the ancient Orthodox view of Christ's death and the modern evangelical view a fundamental difference in the way the word *saved* is being used. This heretical idea of changing God's mind towards the sinner displays a belief that the ultimate difference between those who are saved and those who are not is God's disposition towards them. The truth is that the change is not in God but in us. We are the ones who must leave behind the old life of corruption and embrace the life-filled way of discipleship. We are not seeking Paradise through God's announcement of us as "not guilty" while others still carry a guilty sentence. In this crude model we can quickly understand the Protestant notions of "once saved always saved". But what a dangerous attitude this is. The runner who believes he has already won the race need not train or exert himself any further. There are even some Protestants who believe that to say a particular prayer (and of course mean it!) is to achieve salvation. This mechanical idea, like putting coins into a slot machine and winning salvation, is not to be found in the teaching of the Apostles or the Early Church.

There can be no presumption about our salvation, because it makes a presumption about God's judgement. As we have seen in an earlier chapter, it was that first sin of pride which led to man's downfall. We must remain hopeful because we place ourselves in the hands of a loving God, but we must also continue to be aware of our sins and strive to repent. We all retain free will, and though we may have once committed ourselves to following Christ, all of us are vulnerable to temptation; any of us can fall away. The choices we continue making in our lives are part of the ongoing process.

The Church's true understanding of Christ's death releases us from ideas that God kills in order to punish. This is true both in the case of Christ and for all of us. Whether we mourn for our dead or face impending death ourselves, we must never see it as a sign of God's anger. As has been shown, Christ died to heal us of our sins but also make possible our repentance so that life without sin becomes a new hope for us. The restored image of God within our shared humanity is something we must strive to make real within ourselves, each of us, in lives of obedience.

The Icon Of The Crucifixion

The purpose of the icon of the crucifixion is to help us recognise both the earthly and heavenly aspects of the event. The physical reality of Christ's death is not to be ignored, but at the same time we are to see written into the event the reality that is divine victory over death. The human sorrow of the scene can be recognised in the posture and faces of those who stand looking at the crucified Christ: there before them is the One they believed in, now pierced with a spear and nailed to a cross. The human drama is expressed through the icon because Christ's humanity is suffering death which is common to all mortal men, but the heavenly drama is captured too. In most icons of the crucifixion angels are depicted covering their faces as though mourning the scene before them and yet ready to rush to the soul of Christ who they worship.

But the icon does not dwell on the drama, whether heavenly or earthly, it seeks to point to the meaning of the event. For example we do not see those who mocked Christ and the Roman soldier who performed the brutal act is portrayed suddenly struck by the mystery and wonder of the event. We recognise the Theotokos standing to one side of the cross and Saint John the Apostle to the other: they represent those illuminated by God's truth who stand and see the crucifixion in the way we are now invited to do. Unlike in western art, the crown of thorns is absent because such signs of mockery have no place in the divine nature of the scene. Christ is not a victim; He is not shown at the mercy of His executioners but calmly facing death.

When we look closely we see that Christ's hands are tilted up towards Heaven, His open palms stretched into what could be a moment of praise. But the gesture also extends towards us as an embrace or gesture of welcome and acceptance. In the crucified Christ we see God's open arms extended to all humanity as though He were reaching to hold the whole world. The sense of guilt through which we might look at Him crucified is lifted from us: the very event of which we should be ashamed becomes the means to abolishing our shame. The icon invites us to stand in the presence of the mystery of our salvation, to recognise that Christ came not to condemn sinners but to save us.

In the halo around Christ's head we see the letters O W and V standing for *He Who Is.* Here we see the divine name revealed to Moses from the burning bush, Christ crucified is identified as the God Who spoke to prophets in the Old Testament. Here in the flesh is the God of Genesis, the God of Mount Sinai, the One Who is called YHWH and created all things. God has humbled Himself beyond imagination, even to death on a cross, it is shocking and awe inspiring to behold.

Beneath the cross is depicted a small, dark cave containing a skull. The letters AS indicate that this is the skull of Adam to whom the blood of Christ now flows down to bring salvation. The skull also reminds us that Christ is called the new Adam, where the old Adam brought death through his sin, the new Adam dies to bring life.

On some icons we may also see the letters MG which indicate the Mountain of Golgotha, that place outside the city where the cross was erected. It is shown as nothing more than a small mound while the size of the cross is exaggerated so that it becomes the dominant presence in the image. The cross almost appears to be planted into the earth like a tree, reminding us of that first tree from which sinful man stole fruit, an event overcome through this new tree bearing divine fruit. The cross, even in its brutal ugliness, is venerated as the new tree of Paradise which enables us to enter. As we sing on Good Friday:

Just as the enemy captured Adam with a tree heavy with fruit, so You O lord, captured the enemy with the tree of Your cross and sufferings. Now the second Adam has come to find the one who was lost to restore life to him who was dead.

In some icons there are a number of people shown standing with the Theotokos, the scene is one of a funeral gathering and the characters mourn with God's mother. In contrast to the muted colours of their human sorrow we see Christ shining bright;

death is unable to diminish or contain His glory. He dies on Good Friday, the sixth day of the week, the day in the creation story on which man was first created. He will lie in the tomb for three days reminding us of the Holy Trinity, and rise on the first or symbolically eighth day which represents eternity.

At Pascha we also place a large cloth called the Epitaphios in a tomb of flowers in the centre of the church. On this cloth is embroidered an image of Christ lying dead after the crucifixion. After two days it is placed on the altar where it remains for the Liturgies for the rest of the Paschal season until we reach the day of Ascension. The Epitaphios reminds us of Christ's burial cloths and is a powerful image of the sacrifice that has taken place even when we have moved our focus on to the resurrection.

The icon of the crucifixion draws our hearts back to the death that gives us hope beyond our own. When pain or fear strikes at us, the icon invites us to look beyond our emotions, to recognise God's presence with us as One Who has faced the same darkness. We are invited to see beyond the outward appearance of Christ's death to the reality of God's plan. And we must do the same with the experience of the death of loved ones or our own impending death. Leo the Great encourages us to:

Let the eyes of your mind not dwell only on that sight which those wicked sinners saw but let our understanding, illumined by the Spirit of Truth, foster with a pure and free heart the glory of the cross which irradiates Heaven and earth, and see with inner sight what the Lord meant when he spoke of His coming Passion; "The hour is come that the Son of Man may be glorified."

The same eyes of faith and transformed heart will see the truth beyond our death in this life. We hear many times about the image of the seed planted into the earth. It will rise and from it new life will spring. To the human eye a seed may appear dried and dead, but life is within it. This simple natural reality is given that we may know the truth of death. Our bodies may be lowered into the black soil of the grave, but new life will spring forth.

The Resurrection Of Christ

The resurrection of Christ is the central and essential belief of Christianity. It is not a myth, a fable or a metaphor to be explained away as having some kind of spiritual significance but not to be taken literally. To be a Christian one must absolutely accept that Christ rose from the dead; there are no alternatives if we want to claim membership of Christ's Church.

As Saint Paul wrote:

If Christ has not been raised from the dead, then we have nothing to preach and

you have nothing to believe. (1 Corinthians 15^{14}).

Saint Paul says this because the resurrection of Christ is the fundamental basis of everything we believe. Everything about our faith must crumble if Christ did not rise from the dead. We cannot have a Christ Who is limited to admirable moral teaching or even a worker of miracles remaining overcome by death. Our own life and resurrection is dependant on His victory over this final enemy. If there is no resurrection then we are fools and to be pitied. Countless martyrs have laid down their lives in this faith, our worship takes place on a Sunday in recognition of its reality, every hope and expectation is founded on its truth. But how can Saint Paul have been so sure that death has been destroyed? The answer is that he, like the other

Apostles, had encountered the risen Christ. It was not something they just read about, it was the encounter with Christ Himself that convinced them that He lives. And this must be the basis of our faith too, Christ knocks at the door of our hearts and we can know His risen presence that is our assurance that death has been overcome.

In this chapter we shall consider what it is the Church proclaims and why our holiness is only possible because of the resurrection of Christ. We will see that our own personal perspective on death must be shaped by this reality and that the joyful message of Pascha can and must transform our understanding of life.

It is by Christ's resurrection that God blessed us with eternal life. This is why the liturgies of the Orthodox Church constantly rejoice in and pronounce His resurrection: it is the source of our joy and our hope. Through His resurrection and victory over death Christ makes it possible for the Holy Spirit to descend on to the Apostles and make them the Church. Let us look a little more closely at what the Church Fathers tell us about this supreme event that changed everything.

The nature of our existence has been radically restored by Christ's resurrection. The impact of our sin was on both the material and spiritual nature of man. We can all see the impact of sin on the body: we die. This temporary state continues until the general resurrection of the dead. But the soul too was cast into a state of brokenness that separated it from God. Only through His incarnation, death and resurrection did Christ lift us from the spiritual death that cast the soul of man into darkness when the body died. The Old Testament refers to this condition as Sheol, a place where even the souls of the prophets could not escape. Even to live a life of obedience and seek God's righteousness was not enough to save a man from the terrible consequence of sin. To be separated from God was something no man's efforts could put right, for no man could destroy that final enemy that is death.

Christ's soul descended into Hades while His body lay broken and dead in the tomb. Saint Peter tells us that *He went and preached unto the spirits in prison* (1Peter 3[19]). He descended so that he could raise them up from captivity with Him when he ascended. Saint John Chrysostom in his Homily on Pascha says:

Hell was taken captive by the Lord Who descended into it. It was laid waste, it was mocked, it was put to death, it was overthrown, it was bound.

In this description Saint John teaches us that the very chains of hell have been smashed, it has no claim on us when we are united with the One Who ascends. We are assured that Christ is the first fruit of resurrection, lifting in Himself the fullness of our humanity, our entire human nature. Through Him we are all to be resurrected in our perfected bodies, but for now the righteous enter the Kingdom of God with their King filling the ranks of choirs emptied by the casting out of so many disobedient angels who followed Satan into deceit and corruption.

The resurrection of Christ gives meaning to the joy of Christmas. It would be an unredeemed tragedy if the Church told the story of a perfect child Who was born to die and nothing more. However wonderful the events in between might be, His death could only turn His birth into a defeat. But His resurrection elevates every event in His life to a new level of meaning, every word and miracle is a step towards victory. In the Paschal Matins the Church symbolises the resurrection with the light of a candle held by the priest at the Royal Doors; just as the birth was heralded by the light of a star. A light was lit within humanity and neither the darkness of a tomb or even hell has extinguished it. The light has been poured out amongst us and within us: the divine light of Pascha that shines the way to Heaven, *and the darkness has not overcome it*. Every candle that is lit by the faithful as they enter church is a sign of that resurrection light. It is the fire of Pentecost burning in each of our hearts as we draw closer to that source of resurrection.

We proclaim the light with light, because we have travelled with Christ to Golgotha. The tears of suffering we shed now are preparation for resurrection. Christ called us to *take up our cross and follow Him*, not to meaningless pain, but to the path of resurrection. But we have not yet died, we have not truly passed through crucifixion. We are too often more like the disciples who slept while Christ prayed in Gethsemane than carriers of our own cross. But let us remember that the Holy Spirit descended to the Apostles before their martyrdom: they had not yet achieved the fullness of discipleship but in His mercy God blessed them abundantly. This is our assurance, that though we as yet may know ourselves to be unworthy, Christ does not reject us, His love works in our weakness. We must believe that we are made new in Christ, that the resurrection is more powerful than our willingness to sin, for though it leaves our free will intact, God's love reaches beyond the sin with which we push ourselves from Him.

The evil of our actions is all too clear. We, the human race, had God amongst us; He took our flesh and joined Himself to us. And what did we do? We tortured and killed Him. The insanity of the story is all of our insanity. Every rejection of love and mercy is an action performed under the terrible confusion and spite of this world. And yet the resurrection of Christ is a victory over the worst of it all. It is the gift of eternal life to those who deserve only condemnation. When we take hold of this truth in our hearts there can only be gratitude. The realisation of what God has done for us is the beginning of the resurrection of our own being. We are transformed not at a distance or like a magic trick, but within, through the softening of our angry, stone-hard hearts. We join ourselves to the risen Christ when we allow gratitude to Him to help us see the madness of our judgements of other people. When we are offered so much, how can we possibly hold back anything from those around us? Gratitude to God permits us to recognise how unworthy of His great gift we are and can be a step towards our repentance.

The resurrection of Christ must convince us that we are not here to enjoy clothes and amass riches. Even a healthy body and a long life have no ultimate purpose if at the end of it we die and are forever dead. But we can know eternal life with Christ if we stop living now as dead people, and begin to live as those who truly have eternal life. But to be raised we must die, and so Christians must die to this world. Let us find the right perspective on the cares, concerns and vanities of this world so that we can begin to live for Paradise. We must learn to live for God's approval alone, not the flattery or applause of man. Christ's resurrection is a transforming hope for all of us. Hope that ignites our hearts and which is made real in our Baptism and in the Eucharist. At these times we live out the anticipation of what is to come, and receive His Body and Blood to sustain us until the journey on earth is over. This is why we recognise the worth of this earthly life, because it is the means by which we lay hold of what God offers to us. None of us should forget what a blessing it is to exist and live for this short spell in which we are able to find and accept eternal life in Christ. Every hour and every day is a new opportunity to draw closer and deeper into life, to grow in Christ's image in the power of the Holy Spirit. And every year we sing out in our hymns that Christ has been victorious *Trampling down death by death, and on those in the tombs bestowing life*. It is a proclamation that is ancient, it has rung out on Pascha night through bitter centuries of persecution, from hidden caves and secret churches, to cathedrals and massed choirs. It is the one, same faith in death destroyed that will resonate in the hearts of Christians until the final Second Coming of Christ when all shall be raised. Death is the final enemy because the greatest of human empires, the most exquisite of artworks, the most beautiful of relationships and the richest and fullest experiences of human life are wiped away when man is sent to his grave. This has been the terrible truth for all who live without Christ. Everything must be given up as no more than the fleeting memory of others who themselves will soon follow if life ends with the body's death. It is an all-consuming darkness into which the light of Christ's resurrection shines. Fear of death is crushed beneath faith, love has overcome. Death in this world is the threshold of eternal life. As Saint Gregory of Nyssa proclaims:

The reign of life has begun, the tyranny of death is ended...This is the day the Lord has made – a day far different from those made when the world was first created, and which are measured by the passage of time. This is the beginning of a new creation. On this day, as the prophet says, God makes a new heaven and a new earth.

The Icon of Christ's Descent Into Hell

To help us reflect further on the meaning of Christ's resurrection we will pause for a moment to consider the icon called *The Descent Into Hell* or *The Harrowing Of Hell*. One version of it adorns the front of this book and as you read this chapter I suggest you sometimes look at the details mentioned so that they are able to speak to you from the image.

As a child I saw a western painting of Christ emerging from a tomb, in His hand was a small pendant, and to His sides were two soldiers falling to the ground in amazement and fear. It is quite a striking image and I must admit that onto my impressionable mind it certainly made an impact. But as positive as that impact was it was mixed with a certain amount of sentimentality and didn't lead me any deeper in my reflection of the event. It depicted something I had heard about, and I liked the artist's style. Orthodox icons are very different. While that painting from my youth was an imagined representation of something none of us can ever see, an icon depicts the reality of something that is real and available to us living in the world, it is a painting of theology. The resurrection is not merely a historic event, though it is certainly this, but is a profound experience that can continue to have an impact on us. The icon is an expression of a spiritual reality that can open itself up to those who look at it with an open heart. The icon does not attempt merely to depict the historic event as it might have been observed by someone on the scene, but something that is beyond a single moment in time. The resurrection is an eternal event in that Christ lifts our humanity into eternity, so that our salvation is brought into the here and now with us through the paint and wood. Though icons are not sacraments, there is a similarity in that just as the Eucharist links us with the death and resurrection of Christ, so too spatial removal from the event is overcome as we allow the reality of resurrection to shine out through the icon. This can only be achieved when we approach the icon prayerfully: if we draw near to simply enjoy the artist's skill then we miss its true purpose. The proper approach is made easier when we do so in the context of worship where all our senses are caught up in the act of praising God. This liturgical setting can be echoed in our private and family prayers as we see through the physical object into the spiritual world beyond: the window is in our own hearts and it is not with the physical eyes that we see. The Seventh Ecumenical Council declared that *Whoever venerates an icon, venerates the person it represents.*

Discerning the meaning beyond the seeing we may draw closer to Christ, and so we shall now look at some of the aspects of the icon depicting the resurrection and try to engage with their symbolism. Beneath Christ's feet we see the gates of Hades which have been broken apart and are often shown crossing one another in homage to the means of His death. Below this there are normally keys which seem to float in the abyss; the gates have been torn open by Christ Who has conquered both death and Hades. The gates are no longer locked, the souls within have been granted freedom and they will never be closed again. Our dead do not descend to that place of waiting, there is no place where He is not.

Christ's robes are portrayed flowing upwards to emphasise His powerful descent into the depths of Hades, He rushes to the aid of those who have died, and there is no hesitation or pause. It represents Christ's longing to reach and redeem them for at last God's mighty plan is enacted; the impulse of love urges Him to find them. Christ's clothes are normally white or golden to display the light within Him that transforms even his garments and tells us that He is the Light of the World. Death itself is seen as the skeletal figure that is chained beneath it all. Death has been bound and cast away, or as we chant in our Paschal hymns, Christ is victorious *trampling down death by death*.

The two figures that Christ holds are Adam and Eve being pulled from the darkness. The power of Christ's resurrection is not limited to any one generation; it reaches out to every man who has ever lived. There is no secret place in history where someone is lost to Him, the miracle extends to every part of creation, and through out all time, past, present and future. We see Adam raising his hand; he does not snatch at Christ's hand, but must be lifted by Christ Who grasps him. We too must reach out to Christ believing that He will hold us firmly and carry us heavenwards. Other figures stand to His left, they are the prophets David and Solomon and John the Baptist (still pointing to the Lord). All are family to Christ according to His ancestry, they remind us of God's word spoken by the prophets about this great event, but also signify Christ's own humanity raised up. To the other side of the icon are the Apostles who live, reminding us of this transcendence of time and space. Redemption is an ongoing process that continues to set man free even to the final generation.

Around Christ we see depicted the uncreated light, the same light witnessed by the Apostles at the Transfiguration on Mount Tabor. The light that transforms our darkness into salvation, the light that penetrated the tomb, penetrated Hades and even our black hearts that are so filled with corruption. The light is almond shaped, and so gets its name *Mandorla* from the Italian for almond. It gets progressively darker towards its centre to remind us of the mystery of God, that as we come to know Him we discover the infinite unknown towards which we are eternally called to draw closer.

The harrowing of hell was taught from the beginning of the Church's life, we find it mentioned in the writings of Tertullian just a decade after the event had occurred. The word *harrow* refers to the action of a plough churning and breaking open the soil, just as Christ seems to thrust the cross into Hades.

The icon is a celebration of the divine gift of life. There need be no more fear of death, both Satan and death are bound and imprisoned beneath Christ. Although the devil is still active in our world, the icon encourages us to place all our trust in God, though we must still fight our own battles with evil, the greater victory is accomplished. When the Hebrews surrounded the walls of Jericho they sounded the horns and drums of victory and the walls came tumbling down. We too must face the enemy with hope in Christ's victory, allowing our hope in our salvation to bring it into being in the present.

Christ's body remained wounded and dead in the cold tomb while His soul descended to release those who could not yet enter Paradise. We should be careful not to confuse the word Hades with hell; the former is the place described in the Old Testament where all the dead went, regardless of how righteous or unrighteous they were. The message is that Christ has achieved that which no other man could, only God incarnate is able, it is His final act of self-emptying and abasement: after this there will be only glory. The icon is an image of liberation from all that is symbolised by the cross: suffering, abandonment, fear, rejection and death. The wounds of the cross bleed for every man's wounds, Christ's tears flow for everyone who weeps. And similarly His resurrection is transformation of all who die. The resurrection is the assurance that love is more powerful than anything else in the universe and we must not be afraid to love. In the face of evil we must hold on to the light of resurrection, no matter what the cost or how threatened it makes us feel. Our choosing of love is a manifestation of resurrection, especially when confronted by brutality and hatred. The destruction of the fall has been reversed and humanity is renewed. And so we who grieve or face our own deaths must know that we do not enter the darkness like our distant ancestors. Let us look at the hands of Christ holding Adam and Eve and know that He holds our loved ones in the same way. The icon is not theology for theology's sake but a reminder to us of the truth that must change our attitude towards death. At Matins of the Resurrection we sing:

When You, the immortal Life descended to Death, it was then, that You put Hades to death by the lightning of the Godhead; and when you raised up the dead from the infernal depths. all the

*heavenly powers cried aloud: "O Giver of Life,
Christ our God, glory to You."*

∴THE RES   URRECTION∙

Celebrating Pascha

The Christian celebration of Christ's death and resurrection is the festival that gives meaning to everything else done by Christians; it is the focal point of the whole year. It brings perspective both to faith and all the other Church services but also to our lives and our understanding of our deaths. We will now consider the meaning of the festival as well as how it helps to transform our experience of life as we are drawn into the reality of Pascha.

We should begin with the name. In the West it is usual to call the festival *Easter* whereas the Orthodox tradition uses *Pascha*. This is an important place to start because Pascha is derived from the Hebrew word *Pesach* which most of us translate as *Passover*. Each year Jews celebrate the delivery of the Hebrew slaves from captivity in Egypt. The story involves plagues and miracles, but two details are particularly important for us: the angel of death and the release from slavery. On the night before they were released Moses told the Hebrews to mark their door-posts with the blood of an unblemished lamb so that the angel which God was sending to strike down the first born child would literally pass over their homes. Consequently Pharaoh's resistance was finally overcome as he grieved for his son and the Hebrews were set free.

The early Christians were predominantly Jews who had recognised that the long-awaited Messiah had arrived (a messiah that those who now continue to celebrate the old Passover continue to reject). The story of the Passover was an important aspect of their understanding about how God related to them, it assured them of God's faithfulness and concern, and was a great comfort in difficult times. The death and resurrection of Jesus was always to the Early Church a continuation of how God had revealed Himself, Christianity was not a new religion in that sense, and they knew that Christians were the true inheritors of all that was described in the Old Testament. It was therefore natural that they would interpret all that Christ did in terms of Old Testament theology. Christ Himself had assured them that He was a fulfilment of the Law, that in Him everything that had gone before now came to fruition. We find in Saint John's Gospel Christ referred to as the Lamb of God, the spotless one Who goes without complaint to His death. The Roman soldiers did not break the legs of Jesus as they did the others crucified, this fulfilled the requirement that no bone of the Passover lamb be broken. The physical and spiritual link that Christians make between themselves and Christ's death through Holy Communion is not just a marking of blood on a wooden post, but an inward union of His blood with the body and soul of the communicant. The angel of death passed over on a single night and the children of the Hebrews were protected. Eternal death passes over Christians so that eternal life in all its fullness is granted to them. All will be raised at Judgement, but those who have been transformed (not just marked or outwardly painted) will enter God's blessedness.

We should notice that even for the Hebrews it was not simply a matter of brushing blood over the door in some casual act. It took great courage and faith to do it. If Moses had been wrong, if God had not been faithful, Pharaoh could have sent his soldiers round the following morning identifying all the troublemakers by the blood on their doorposts. This is still true for Christians today. The demands of discipleship are not a single action, a particular prayer or even participation in a single sacrament, discipleship makes demands on us, it requires us to take risks, it is only real when we place all our hope and trust in God. And in doing so Christians experience the second feature of the Passover which is Exodus from the slavery; release from sin and death.

Therefore we can see that the name *Pascha* is important because it links Christian practice with this earlier tradition. In fact many scholars have argued that the western term *East*er is derived from an Anglo-Saxon pagan Goddess called *Eostre*. While some fundamentalists will react with horror at such a claim or else become hostile to the western term, we should remember that this is an indication of how early Christian missionaries would use the terms and ideas of those they were evangelising in order to make the Christian faith more accessible and is not a definitive sign that anyone who uses the term is somehow unduly influenced by paganism.

The celebration of Pascha is not akin to a historical recreation society, Christians are not focussed on the events of Christ's death and resurrection as distant memories, however important, which are worthy of remembrance and nothing else. Pascha enables Christians to enter into the experience of those events in a profound way so that the saving passion and life-giving resurrection become a living hope that transforms the present reality. The chronology of the historical events provide a framework through which Christians pass, the encounters and actions of Christ in the week before His death and resurrection were divinely orchestrated so that over thousands of years Christians would be drawn deeper into their meaning and purpose. Words spoken to Apostles or Pharisees reach across countless generations touching hearts in whatever condition they may be in.

Holy Week begins with Christ's entry into Jerusalem on what is called Palm Sunday. The mood is triumphant, a brief moment of celebration in the austere days of Lent. Christ permits the crowds to welcome Him with cheers, but many of those same voices will be crying out *Crucify Him* in less than a week. We discover a warning to us that even those who enjoy worship and genuinely celebrate Christ's name can be misled and come to reject Him. As we pass through this brief life we must work hard to guard ourselves from becoming one of the crowd which only accepts Christ on our terms according to our conceptions of who God is.

After a series of four Bridegroom services where we remind ourselves of the incarnation and how God has become one of us we move through Holy Week to Holy Thursday. On this night we contemplate the Last Supper and through a number of gospel readings begin our journey through the passion of Christ. The solemnity of the festival begins to affect our sense of time and space, laughter and superficiality suddenly become out of place, we are touched by the seriousness of our own existence and our place before Almighty God.

On Good Friday we focus through the Royal Hours on Christ's suffering on the cross. Our own suffering in life takes on a new meaning; we begin to grasp the connection between our experiences and God's plan for us. As we focus on a tomb erected in the centre of the church we draw close to the reality of death. But even here the Church does not present a stark and hopeless image. The tomb is decorated with flowers, its cold reality contains a glimpse of the coming resurrection, even when confronted by the stone cave where His body was laid, we cannot see defeat. Unlike His followers at the time our journey through this event is always in the knowledge of what is to come. And this is the message we must all hold onto in the hours of pain and death that we face. With hindsight we know where Christ's passion leads. But it is the same hindsight that we must apply to our own life. Hope and faith become a new hindsight for us all; we do not suffer without knowing of the resurrection: How much comfort the Apostles would have had if they had known what was to come. In this sense our experience is easier because we have that comfort. Their grief is recognised in the service of Lamentations when we carry the tomb beyond the doors of the church. In a form of funeral procession we draw close to the Theotokos as she mourns over her son, her faith so pure that she maintains hope even without the hindsight granted to us. For mothers who mourn their children she is a great comfort and her prayers are always to be sought.

Holy Saturday begins with a Divine Liturgy in which the priest scatters leaves over the floor. The power of Christ has broken through the great gates of Hades and the people will stamp over all that has accumulated against them. Later as we approach midnight the image of light pierces the darkened church in a single candle carried through the Royal Doors by the priest. The iconostasis represents the division between earth and Heaven, and this light comes forth as a sign of the miracle that begins with God but passes to all mankind. The congregation pass the flame amongst them, each carrying a candle to proclaim that the resurrection of one has brought light to all. From the darkness of a tomb has sprung forth eternal life for all humanity, and at last we are able to sing *Christ is Risen.* The immediacy and personal meaning of this moment is shared by the faithful, it is a gift each knows as though they were the only human alive but it is also the declaration of our shared humanity not only with Christ but also with each other. It is a moment filled with joy that unites Christians beyond the individual moments of death each of us must face.

When we look at the writings of the Early Church we recognise an anticipation of the imminent return of Christ. This world will not continue as it is for much longer and they lived accordingly. It is worth noting that the time of Christ is not so far from us even in this age. If we take a fifty year old man, then we only need a chain of forty such men to cover the entire period from Christ to us at the beginning of the twenty first century. If we imagine just forty men in a row we get a proper sense of how close that time really is. The early Christians were not deluded; they had a view of reality we should all aspire to share. Certainly for each of us personally the end of this world is closer than we think, but as for the whole world none of us knows the hour. Pascha is the traditional time for baptism because it marks our move from death to life. We move from onlookers to participants in the Paschal events through our baptism. And so we should become those who like the Jews looked for the coming messiah to those who look for the second coming of Christ.

All worship is an encounter with God, it is here that the Holy Spirit living within the Church makes God's presence known to us just as Jesus promised to be with two or three gathered in His name. It does not matter whether it is a packed cathedral or a hermit's cave where a few monks meet to pray, the Church's worship is gathered to be with the heavenly worship of the angels. Therefore we should acknowledge that at the pre-eminent service of all the Church's acts of worship God makes His presence known to us. Not in visions or altered states of consciousness, Christians do not seek anything of this sort, but in the tangible sense of God being there. This is because Pascha is specifically focussed on our redemption; it is liturgical entry into our salvation.

Pascha offers great comfort to those in mourning and reassurance to those with a clear sense of their mortality. To be gathered in celebration in the face of death is a decisive blow against Satan. Pascha denies his power over us, it is the fore-taste of an eternal feast which is already tasted in faith. Pascha is our declaration that death is overcome, that no matter how dark or painful this life becomes we have already begun to celebrate with those in Heaven. Pascha removes us from the shackles of time as we know it and allows us to touch eternity.

Christ Raised Others

On three occasions in the gospels we read of Christ raising other people from the dead: the widow of Nain's son, Jairus' daughter and Lazarus. Each of these miraculous events has something to teach us but they also reveal a great truth collectively. They reveal to us both the heavenly power of Christ but also His humanity.

In the seventh chapter of Saint Luke's Gospel we read about Christ entering a town called Nain. As he passes through He meets a funeral procession and sees a widow mourning the death of her only son. Christ's response is one of compassion; He is moved by her situation and her grief and decides to intervene. Touching the funeral cart he instructs the dead man to sit up and immediately the widow's son does so and begins to speak. Saint Luke tells us that amongst the crowd there were many who were filled with fear at what they had seen while others began to praise God. The miracle shakes those whose beliefs do not permit such an act of God while those who believe are given comfort and assurance by what Christ has done.

When we look closely at Christ's actions we see that He has no social or personal connection with the widow, but reacts simply out of concern for her. The miracle is an encouragement to us all to believe that God cares about the pains and sorrows of our lives, we are important to Him. The gospels tell us that Christ raised the man and *delivered* him to his mother. This is important because it shows that Christ has taken possession of the dead man, he belongs to Christ Who hasn't simply restored or raised him, but has claimed him as His own. In His compassion He then gives the son back to the mother. As we shall see, it is the same compassion that Christ demonstrates each time He raises someone from the dead: these miraculous signs although they have further meaning, are primarily an act of love.

In the case of Jairus' daughter there is a further message. When Christ approaches the scene of a young girl's death He assures the servants and family that she is only sleeping: their response is to laugh at Him. It seems to them that all hope has been lost, that death has removed any reason to believe that anything more can be done. The miracle teaches us to trust in God even beyond logic or what might seem to make sense. Taking the girl by the hand Christ overcomes the darkness and tenderly calls her to life.

The third person to be raised from the dead is Christ's friend Lazarus. In this case there is much greater symbolism at work and each year the Church commemorates the event on the Saturday before Palm Sunday: it is the feast before we begin our journey through Holy Week. The Church recognises it as the prophetic sign that points to

Christ's own resurrection, it is a triumphant miracle that helps the Apostles and us prepare for Pascha Sunday. It does this by establishing Christ's power and supporting the reality of God's intention to overcome death. It is no accident that following Lazarus Saturday Christ's entry into Jerusalem is celebrated as a brief moment of earthly recognition of Christ's identity.

The raising of Lazarus also points to the general resurrection that is to come. In the conversation between Christ and Lazarus' sister Martha, we hear Him linking the raising of Lazarus with what will happen to every one of us. Martha acknowledges her belief in the coming resurrection of all. Christ then explicitly links this with himself: *I am the resurrection* He says. He does not say *I will bring the resurrection* or *I will make the resurrection happen*, but *I am the Resurrection*. The power over death is within Him because He is life. Christ is revealing that life does not end in death, the dead live on in Christ, it is in Him that we live now and on into eternity. Martha's error is in limiting her concept of resurrected life to a distant point in the future. She does not see that all that she hopes for lives and stands before her in Christ. It is near to her as it is near to all of us in Him.

Christ raises each of these three people at different stages in the process of death and burial, His authority reaches into every place of being. First we see Jairus' daughter has just died and is still lying on her bed. The widow of Nain's son has been dead for more time and is being carried to his burial. And finally Lazarus is already in his tomb. For the Jews the delay of four days before Christ raised Lazarus would have particular significance because amongst some of them there is the tradition that the soul remains close to the body for three days but then leaves: Christ's miracle reaches deep into the reality of death for them. The Church Fathers teach us that each of these three stages represents spiritual death not just physical death. The redemptive power of Christ brings life to sinners; the raising of the dead is similar to the conversion of sinners: both are a release from a form of bondage. The raising of Lazarus should give all sinners hope since it demonstrates that no matter how spiritually dead we may feel, no matter how long we feel we have laid in the tomb, Christ can still reach us. For some people this kind of spiritual resurrection may seem as impossible and foolish as did the idea that Jairus' daughter was able to return to those who mourned. But the power of God is made clear in these events and we should know that it can overcome the deadest of hearts.

The Church understands the raising of these three in a different way to the form of resurrection that will occur before the judgement of all. These individuals were raised in bodies which were still destined to die; the period of life which they were raised for would come to an end with biological death just like everyone else's life does. They were not resurrected in the way that Christ will raise everyone at the end of time, and neither did they experience death in the way that we who die since the resurrection of Christ do. For example, Saint Lazarus, who went on to be appointed by Saints Stephen and Barnabas as the first bishop of what is now Larnaca in Cyprus, was said to have been deeply affected by his experience of death (he had fled from Bethany because the Jews had made plans to murder him because he was such a powerful witness to the faith of the Christians). He lived for another thirty years after Christ had raised him and was said to have had a very sober personality because of his memory of the unredeemed in Hades. The place of the dead was still holding them tightly in its bonds and death itself was still a cause of terrible fear. It is not too extreme to say that sin and death still ruled over man, death plunged humanity into the tyranny of hopelessness despite the Jewish teaching on the general resurrection. The dead experienced a state of rejection; unable to be united with God they knew a spiritual death. But the death Lazarus would experience after the resurrection of Christ was a victory and passage to something better.

It is interesting to note that in the gospel account of Christ's raising of Lazarus the miracle does not occur immediately after Christ has prayed. Following his shedding of tears and words of prayer, Christ speaks differently: we glimpse His authority. He commands *Lazarus, come out*! Saint John Chrysostom recognises in Christ's words not just a command to His friend, but an order given to death itself. Also we should note that the command to Lazarus was not to *rise from the dead*, but to *come out*! Christ speaks directly to one who has not ceased to exist, Lazarus is held in the tomb by death and he must come out from the darkness of both. Lazarus was called by name because he retained his identity; death did not strip him of being the person God had created him to be. But also we recognise the voice of Christ calling to one man at this moment: His command could so easily have raised all those in the tombs around them. But this was not yet the time for all men to be resurrected when the great trumpet blast will call us forth as Christ's shout did Lazarus. Christ's shout also reminds us that in less than a week there would be other voices raised in shouts: the crowd calling for His crucifixion.

The onlookers saw Lazarus walk out of the tomb still shrouded in his burial cloths. Christ has raised him in the full physicality of his being, not as some cleaned up image of himself. These were the strips with which Martha and Mary had bound his body. The impact of seeing life within those bandages must have reinforced the reality of what they were seeing: after all, the God who can release a soul from Hades can surely untie the body from a few cloths. But Lazarus stands before them in the full clothing of death; Christ's power has gone beyond both death and the rituals of men. The burial chants and prayers that accompanied him to the grave have been transformed into hymns of praise.

Can any of us imagine how sweet the voice of Christ must have sounded to one who was bound in Hades? The voice of life entered the darkness in response to the voices of Mary and Martha who shouted from their own place of darkness. When grief envelops us it can be like every light has been extinguished. But the story of Lazarus reminds us that we must call out as did his sisters, we must pray in faith no matter how impenetrable the darkness around us feels. Secondly we must hear that same sweet voice calling to us no matter how dark our lives may feel. We may have entombed ourselves in sin, we may be shrouded in grief, but Christ calls us by name. But like Mary and Martha who sent a message to Christ of their brother's illness but had to wait four days before He came, we must wait with the patience of faith. Christ promises to reunite us with our loved ones, just as the family of Martha, Mary and Lazarus was restored, our family ties have not come to an end at death.

To discover new life in Christ is to be possessed by Him as the widow's son became His possession. We belong to Christ when we live in Him; our slavery is freedom from the bondage of death. We live in a different age to Lazarus, for now death's claims on us are destroyed. The joys we hope to experience with God could not have been known by him. Therefore when we lose someone we must ask ourselves whether we would truly want to call them back to meet the demands and pains of this world instead of the blessedness that we pray they enjoy in Christ. Our patience is not for the arrival of the One Who will call our loved ones from the grave, but for the final day when we shall all be resurrected. The brief time between bereavement and our own death is the blink of an eye, the few days we must carry our cross are nothing compared to eternity. So let us remain steadfast in our trust in God and hold on to the promise Christ gives to all of us:

Whosoever liveth and believeth in me shall never die.

The Soul After Death

Earlier we saw that the teaching of the Church is and has always been that when the soul leaves the body at the moment of physical death it remains conscious of itself and its surroundings. To reflect further on what happens to the soul we will consider additional evidence from the Bible and consider how Saint John Damascene and others add to our understanding. A proper grasp of what happens to us and our loved ones can help us overcome our fear: so often it is the unknown that fuels the fearful imagination.

The Bible is clear that the souls of the righteous enjoy the blessings of God after death. In Hebrews we read of *the spirits of just men made perfect* (Hebrews 12^{23}) who surround Jerusalem with the angels. Saint Paul believed that the Church in Heaven live with Christ, awaiting His Second Coming when they will receive their perfected bodies.

In a sense it would be unthinkable that God would have no plan for us between our death and the final Judgement. Just as we believe that death cannot end the love we feel for each other, then how much more can we be assured that God's love is eternal. The soul is the essence of who we are, it could not lose the God-given capacities to think and perceive just because it has been separated from the earthly body. The Church teaches that at death we each undergo what is called a "particular" judgement, something that takes place immediately when we die. As Saint Paul writes: *It is appointed that man will die once, but after this the judgement* (Hebrews 9[27]). Saint Paul speaks separately of the General Judgement of all mankind, the final reward or punishment of each of us is yet to come, but our dead have a foretaste of their eternal reward even now.

The Church does not specify in dogma many details of this particular judgement, what we have are the divinely inspired descriptions provided by the saints and theologians, but we must read with care, since what is sometimes written in allegory to help us grasp something of the mystery must not be taken always as a literal explanation. We know from these that the angels of God and the fallen angels of Satan will defend and attack us, this is supported many times in the Bible. For example in the parable of Lazarus and the rich man Christ tells us that Lazarus was *carried by the angels* to be with Abraham in Heaven just as He also tells us that at the end of time the angels will be sent to separate the *wicked from the just*.

The demons attempt to lay claim to the souls of the dead in accordance with the life that the person lived while the angels serve to protect them. For those who have lived without concern for their judgement this will be a terrible shock to discover that they are now prey to the evil spirits they have been serving through out their life. In life we incline ourselves to participate in good or evil, our soul is joined to the work of God or that of Satan, and so it is not surprising that when we die we will still move towards one or the other. It must be made clear that we believe that the demons have no sovereignty over the righteous (those who are united to Christ). There are passions of soul and body, and even the former are often enacted through the body. After death the soul which is filled with passions can no longer satisfy itself and these unfulfilled passions stifle and injure the soul. The demons, which we can choose to give authority over us, can only act on the soul by means of these passions. And so by repentance, a certain amount of asceticism and participating in the sacramental life of the Church a person is able to slowly cut off these harmful impulses: this is the healing spoken of in an earlier chapter.

What happens after death has been written about in great depth, but here we must note our earlier caution. To completely describe such spiritual mysteries is impossible in worldly analogies; the images we use will always fall short of the reality. It requires a level of spiritual discernment that few of us are equipped with to see the inner meaning of these images, and so what follows must be understood in the context of this warning. We are not describing the literal events as they happen but attempting to see into their meaning through imagery.

Saint John Maximovitch was a twentieth century bishop who used the language of days to describe the soul's journey. We can immediately see that the language is meant to be interpreted allegorically since the soul leaves the world of time measured in days once it enters eternity. He tells us that for two days after death the soul experiences a certain amount of freedom during which time it is able to come to terms with its new state and reflect on the life that it has led. But on the third day it must meet evil spirits which confront it with the various temptations that it faced in life. Some writers have referred to these temptations as being like *toll houses*, that is, points through which the soul must be tested before it can continue. Some writers have mistakenly attributed a literal interpretation to the toll houses and created a vision of the soul's journey that is too terrible to contemplate. But the warning contained in the idea must not be discarded because of this error. Saint John Maximovitch is warning us that after death we will have to face the consequences of our choices here on earth. This is judgement; it is as though our inner condition is finally observable in all its truth. The evils we happily perform in this life are the attractions we feel to demonic influences. These attractions will continue to pull at us and if we have not repented then we are warned they can pull us away from the path to God. The soul's journey after death reflects the use of our free will in this life, but becomes powerless to choose, it reaps the seeds sown in life before death.

The image must be understood in its historic context. For many in the early centuries of the Church the tax collector had gained his reputation not just because he took more than he was supposed to, but because they had a reputation for meddling. While searching for hidden goods tax collectors were known to rifle through people's freight, investigating private belongings. They were seen as an oppressive force whose enquiries were resented. It was this familiar idea that the Church Fathers were using to describe what happens to us after death. It is an image that warns us that the souls of the unrepentant are subject to unwanted influence beyond their control.

The soul that passes beyond these temptations is described by Saint John as then visiting various realms of both Heaven and hell. He describes the soul seeing the reality of both habitations but not yet knowing which will be his reward. The tradition is that this period lasts for forty days, and the Church teaches us that during this period the prayers of the living are particularly beneficial to the dead, bringing them great comfort. It is also important that the dead are commemorated at the Divine Liturgy by the priest, for there are numerous accounts of saints who have been assured in visions that these prayers are more powerful than any other. We believe that while the serving of panikhidas brings comfort to our dead, the prayers at the Liturgy have the greatest impact of all. We must all pass the names of our loved ones to our priest for commemoration so that as he mixes the particles of Christ's Body and Blood they are granted relief. The world tells us that we must have lavish parties and expensive gravestones, but none of this benefits those we love. The Church understands that it is most important to pray for them during that initial forty day period.

Saint John of Damascus writes:

O Virgin, in the hour of death rescue me from the hands of demons, and the judgement, and the accusations, and the frightful testing, and the bitter toll houses and the fierce prince, and the eternal condemnation, O Theotokos.

Again we find here the immediate judgement after death, and it is clearly linked with the image of the toll houses. It is perhaps helpful to see them in terms of testing. Judgement is not a superficial announcement of good or bad, but an unwrapping of the deepest secrets of who we are. It is the revealing of those hidden sins which we persist in, the evil that we allow to mould our soul. In this way we can understand the toll houses as an image of the various stages of our judgement, a way to understand that it will be a process of revelation which will be painful and bitter. The toll houses should be something that prompts us to resist the demons in this life, for every act of repentance now protects and frees us at judgement. While the descriptions of the toll houses depict the demons accusing us, in fact it is we who determine our fate after death in the lives we are living.

In this pattern of days the soul arrives at a completion of the process on the fortieth day and enters into the foretaste of either Heaven or hell. But the Church maintains that even at this point and on until the day of the General Resurrection the soul still benefits from our prayer. The state of the soul can change, since the final judgement which seals the condition of all for eternity has not yet taken place. This is why there is always hope, we must never give up on our dead, no matter how lost they may have seemed in life. The fact that the Church prays for the dead is also a rejection of the heretical idea considered earlier that the soul enters a state of sleep: our belief that prayers are beneficial to the dead is a sign that they are in an active state which can be affected by us.

A criticism of the idea of the toll houses has been that it seems to place our particular judgement in the hands of the demons. However, Seraphim Rose equates the toll houses with ascetic struggles in life, a form of testing rather than a reward or final punishment. In this way we can see that what happens to the soul after death has much in common with what happens in life. Not just in the consequences of that life, but in the similarity between the two experiences of temptation. The main difference, however, is that the Fathers universally warn us that in this life we are able to repent, but after death there can be no repentance. Just as in this life, the soul that is united to Christ has greater protection in the spiritual warfare, so too the soul after death must wear its armour and carry its shield if it is to defend itself from the arrows of the enemy's army. Saint Dorotheos warns us that:

The thoughts he speaks of are those of this world, about houses and possessions, parents and children, and business transactions. All these things are destroyed immediately when the soul passes out of the body. But what he did against virtue or against his evil passions, he remembers and none of this is lost. In fact, the soul loses nothing that it did in the world but remembers everything at its exit from the body.

It will be far worse to remember the terrible things we have done and be powerless to change them than it is to remember death and judgement while we live and have time to repent. The attractions of this life call out to us; the laughter of this world insists that we deny such thoughts as morbid and unnecessary. It is a struggle, particularly in this modern age when life is full of artificial delights, to overcome our inclination to ease and self-will. But the struggle we enter now will be our victory when the soul leaves the body. To live on we must die now. We must put to death the passions, take up our cross and crucify the old man of sin, that we may also be resurrected now in the new life of Christ. For it is this new life of the Spirit that will sustain us when the body dies. The toll houses are a further symptom of sin, and the perfect life of Christ within us overcomes every demonic charge. But when we understand that even the souls of the righteous still feel fear (though they will be protected and according to Saint Gregory the Theologian, know an immediate sense of gladness and peace at death), how much more terrifying must it be for those who die unrepentant. We should scrutinise ourselves long before this other terrible scrutiny begins. The Fathers speak of the soul at the hour of death like a besieged city: we must secure its defences while there is time. The hours before death are particularly important in this. While modern medical practice offers great physical relief to the dying, modern drugs can impair the dying person's ability to seek God's mercy. We should all pray that when it comes to our death we are granted that vital time to reflect and repent. Saint John Chrysostom describes this vividly: *sins contort his soul, they stir up the soul.*

The desire of the man-hating demons is to prevent us reaching Heaven. The analogy is that they tax the soul, making demands of it according to its condition. But their mouths utter slander too and in some accounts of the death of saints we see God's holy ones refuting false accusations at their death as the demons draw near to try and take hold of them. Saint Anthony the Great described a vision of the devil at his door holding back the souls of the dead from proceeding to Heaven while other souls peacefully ascended to be in Paradise. It is a fearful thought but we must not allow it to cause despondency. Christ offers to arm us now by calling us to repent of jealousy, lust, greed, pride and so on. All those passions which the demons seek to stir up in us must be cast off through repentance and prayer. None of us faces death entirely free of sin, all fall short. And so we see that salvation is only possible through God's mercy. None of us should see ourselves beyond His love, no matter how vile our sin. Similarly we should never assume that our dead are beyond God's mercy either. Without His willingness to forgive none of us could reach Heaven. So God does not expect us to be perfect, but He does expect us to repent. This is the essential aspect of the soul that will rise with the angels. We sin, but we must repent, confess our sins and try to do better. When we sin again we repent once again, and so on. This is the work of the soul that must be accomplished before death. The thief who died beside Christ at the crucifixion acknowledged his sins and asked Christ's forgiveness. It is his act of repentance for which Christ rewards him.

At this stage it is important to consider the souls of infants after death. Unlike the Roman Catholic and Protestant groups the Church does not believe that we inherit the guilt of Adam, only the consequences of his sin. While Roman Catholics consider a new-born infant sinful since it shares in Adam's guilt, the Orthodox teach that we inherit only the fruit of sin which is death. This is why Orthodox families are not in such a rush to baptise their babies, although too much of a delay is to be avoided so that the child can receive Holy Communion. This difference is important because the cruelty of Roman theology can leave bereaved parents with the fear that their dead child may not be with God. Let us firmly reject such heresy, Saint John Chrysostom writes that in answer to the accusations of the demons the infants will sing:

The dark custom officials saw our body spotless and were put to shame, they saw the soul good and pure and were embarrassed: they saw the tongue immaculate and they were silenced.

Christ commands us to be like little children. Not naive and ignorant, but spotless and with mouths empty of lies, blasphemy or curses.

We cannot give a full explanation of exactly where the soul dwells after death, in what Saint John Chrysostom calls the *uncrowned* state prior to the crowning of the Final Judgement, but we must trust that God's will for us is infinitely better than anything we could fantasise about. Christ has given us everything sufficient to take away our fear and guide us safely to our home with God. If we trust, believe and try to be obedient, Christ will not dessert us. What we must take from these images is a seriousness with which we must prepare for death. We must abandon everything that we know is destructive to the soul, everything that is contrary to the Christian life. The idea of the toll houses is not a form of purgatory where the soul is somehow cleansed, but a way to express the examination of our life and choices. But ultimately it is not individual good or bad acts which save or condemn us. It is the soul that sins and repents and joins itself to Christ which is victorious. The ruler of this world has no power over Christ or those who belong to Him. As Saint Symeon assures us *He who has God's light conquers the demons that come near him.* The light of Christ within us overcomes the prince of darkness.

The General Resurrection

At the beginning of creation God created space and time within which every moment of our lives is contained. Our language, images, thoughts and perceptions exist within this created order. When we are in communion with God we meet the One Who is beyond time (He existed *before* time and made time – though here we see the limits of language because we cannot conceive of what being before time means). History unfolds along the linear passage of time, one event following another, and as it passes we grow old and die. But time is not eternity (and eternity is not just lots of time), just as it had a beginning so it races towards its end. The end of time will mark the end of this existence as we know it and God will introduce those things that revelation has made known to us. There will be a resurrection and judgement of all people, and we will each enter the condition of either Heaven or hell described in a later chapter.

Christ was resurrected in His body, as we have seen He was not a ghost without physical form. So too our resurrection will be in the flesh. Since the soul is immortal, and death is really the separation of soul and body, then we can understand the general resurrection as the reuniting of our souls and bodies. But whereas the human body was once corruptible it will be raised incorruptible by God.

For those who have united themselves with Christ, this will be a moment of great blessing, as Saint Ephraim the Syrian says:

The graves will open, and in the twinkling of an eye all of the tribes will be awakened and will look upon the holy greatness of the Bridegroom. Great multitudes of Angels and Archangels, countless armies, will rejoice with great joy; the saints, the righteous, and all who had not accepted the seal of the ungodly serpent, will rejoice. All who had been hiding in caves, will rejoice together with the Bridegroom in the eternal and heavenly mansions with all the saints unto ages of ages.

We find belief in the General Resurrection in both the Old and New Testaments as well as in the writings of the Church Fathers. In Genesis we hear God saying to Noah that *the bodies of dead men will rise again* and Isaiah writes:

The dead shall rise again, and they that are in the graves shall awake, and it is clear that the souls do not lie in the grave but the bodies.

In the gospels we have a clear indication that Christ taught that the resurrection of the dead will include their bodies. He said:

They that are in the graves shall hear His voice and shall come forth: they that have done good unto the resurrection of life, and they that have done evil unto the resurrection of damnation (John 5[28-29]).

And in the writings of the early Church Fathers we see this faith made clear:

The souls of Christians go to an invisible place designated by God for them and remain there until the final resurrection. Afterwards, after receiving bodies and rising again perfectly (i.e. with their bodies) just as our Lord Himself rose, they will come to the sight of God.

As we have already observed, the raising of Lazarus was a sign of the nature of resurrection, both of Christ and us, but it also shows that the body being resurrected will not be a new one, it will be these same bodies but transformed. Therefore we should see our resurrection to be the reunion of soul and body that God first joined together in creation. Just as we understand Christ's action of dying as joining Himself with our death, so now we see He Who is incorruptible united with our corruption. The perfection of our physical being depends as much on Christ's resurrection as does our inner union with God. Christ conquered death but also all corruption. If death is the fruit of sin, then we must see the corruptible state of our bodies as having the same cause. Through His destruction of sin He has opened the door to our own physical restoration. When Christ encountered disbelief in such resurrection amongst the Jewish Sadduccees He condemned their lack of faith and knowledge of the scriptures.

So let us consider what we know of this resurrection. First we are taught that it will be universal. Every man who has ever lived will rise, from every age and from every place in the earth. Regardless of race, religion or age, all will stand to face Christ, whether they are sinners or saints. Anyone who teaches that only specific groups will rise or that the righteous will rise separately is in error. However, the condition that sinners find themselves raised in will be different from those united to Christ. Saint Ephraim warns that when resurrected, some of us *will resemble light and others darkness*. In our resurrected form the inner reality of our hearts will be clear, all will be known and seen, nothing will be in secret any longer.

This universal nature of the resurrection leads to the second dogma which is that the resurrection will be simultaneously experienced everywhere in the world. At the Coming of Christ He will not visit different places at different times, which is why there will never be any need for others to tell us that He has arrived. Christ warned that in the end times there will be those who seek to mislead or confuse people by announcing that Christ has returned. No such announcement will be necessary. The whole world will see Him in an instant, and in the same moment the dead will rise.

The nature of our bodies is touched on a number of times both in scripture and by the Fathers. What we can say is that the body we have now will be the body that is transfigured; it is the same you and I that are raised, since it is the soul and body which make us who we are. A completely different body would not be resurrection and it would not be the same us. But when Saint Mary saw Christ in the garden she mistook Him for the gardener. We can certainly say that there is a certain symbolic meaning in this event, since the resurrected Christ is perceived in one sense to be like Adam in Eden who was given the garden to care for. And again it may be that amidst the anxiety of that weekend when He was crucified and having discovered His body not to be in the tomb, she may not have been psychologically prepared for the encounter. However, the event does seem to point to a change in Christ that did not make Him immediately recognisable. Similarly the disciples who walked with Him on the road to Emmaus did not recognise Him as He walked with them and explained the meaning of the scriptures about Himself to them. And yet when He invited Saint Thomas to touch the wounds of crucifixion on His body it is clear that the signs where He had been marked by the nails and the spear were still visible. It is useful to reflect on these details but we mustn't attempt to explain them fully since there is a deeper mystery here that cannot be dissected too far. In the garden Christ instructed Saint Mary not to touch Him because He had not yet ascended to the Father, a further aspect which adds to the miraculous nature of the event but which we should be wary of falling into speculation about.

Therefore we can at least say with certainty that our bodies will be the same ones but made incorruptible. This means that they will no longer be subject to sickness or fatigue, they will be immortal and free from the restraints and weaknesses that are experienced in this world. The bodies of those who have rejected Christ will also be raised incorruptible, but will express the inner state of the soul.

The raising of our bodies is not affected by the physical condition or location of our remains here on earth. There are many saints whose bones are treasured in different parts of the world: this in no way implies that God cannot gather together that which is necessary for a perfected body. Similarly there are examples of martyrs whose bodies have been divided by persecutors, or crushed in the jaws of wild beasts in the arena. In our secular world there are countless bodies which are given over to the ovens of crematoria and their remains sometimes scattered to the wind. While this treatment of the dead is entirely unchristian (see later chapter) it in no way interferes with the power of God Who created our bodies out of dust and Who will do so once again.

The General Resurrection is beyond anything man has known in this life. As a result the Apostles turned to images from nature to express its reality.

They write of seeds planted in the earth which appear dead but spring forth in fresh, green life. However we perceive it, we should know that God has revealed this future event to us so that none of us should be caught by surprise. The actual hour of its occurrence is unknown, but this is a blessing. If we were to know of a specific date too many of us would feel a false sense of time, like a teenager who leaves his examination revision to the last hour, believing that all that is necessary can be accomplished before the test. But this would be an entirely misguided understanding of what is to come. We must use whatever lifespan God gives us to begin the process of theosis. For those who will rejoice at their resurrection that which will be perfected in an instant will be the completion of what had already begun in life. But above all we should know that our loving God has given us knowledge of what is to come so that we may be prepared and rewarded. It gives us a proper perspective on the things of this world and particularly on the human body. Those of us stricken with disease or born with disabilities must carry this burden only for a little while. We must not grow to resent the body God has given us; it will be perfected and made the true servant of our soul. We can begin its transformation by denying its impulses that are contrary to God's will. Small acts of self-denial such as prescribed in the Church's calendar of fasts help us to take control of the body. As we overcome its urges to overeat, seek inappropriate sexual pleasures or become lazy then we participate in that perfecting that God will complete at our resurrection. If the soul is enslaved by the body then resurrection will be torment because it will be reunion with a tyrant.

Judgement

The Final Judgement should be a fearful prospect for everyone. Those who feel confident about it are in a state of delusion and need to wake up. Some of the holiest saints have quaked at the thought of God's Final Judgement, for their nearness to God has made them all too aware of their sins. Those who feel they have little to worry about do not have the Holy Spirit Who convicts us inwardly through our conscience. As our holiness grows so too does the awareness of our own wickedness: it is not pious rhetoric or artificial humility when the saints refer to themselves as the greatest of all sinners for in their spiritual maturity they see only the good in others and no virtue of their own. So let none of us imagine that judgement will not be painful as we stand before Almighty God without any means of hiding our sins. But at the same time we must never lose hope since it is through our union with Christ our perfect Saviour that we will be able to look at the glory of God and rejoice. The Final Judgement is the end of the world: this does not mean its destruction because like our bodies it will be renewed.

In this chapter we will consider how the event is depicted in scripture and how the Church Fathers have made this revelation accessible to us. We will also look carefully at the signs that Christ has commanded us to look for that will indicate its nearness.

The Bible refers to the Final Judgement many times; its importance makes it a recurring theme particularly in the gospels and the letters of Saint Paul. In Matthew we find Christ giving a vivid description of what will happen, he says:

When the Son of man comes in His glory, and all the angels with Him, then He will sit on His glorious throne. Before Him will be gathered all the nations and He will separate them one from another as a shepherd separates the sheep from the goats (Matthew 25[31-33]).

Christ goes on to explain that this separation will be according to how men have treated one another, how much they have loved. As we have said elsewhere it is the outward manifestation of the inner transformation that these acts of love represent. It is the inner disposition, the state of a man's soul that will cast him to the left or right. When we look at this image we are struck immediately by a number of details. The judgement will be universal, every nation will stand before Him, and yet it will also be personal and individual as He distinguishes one from another. No one will escape it and at the same time the depth of scrutiny will be as though we were the only one standing before Him. How joyful will those people be who have confessed the stain on their heart in this life before Christ calls them to account.

Saint John Chrysostom reminds us that like the sheep and the goats we live together, unaware of who is a sheep or a goat. In Palestine it is still possible to see sheep that resemble goats; they are not the carefully bred creatures roaming western hillsides that can be distinguished from goats at a glance. Therefore it is not up to us to begin trying to judge who is who, we live together, as Saint John Chrysostom says:

For now we are not separated, but all mingled together, but the division then shall be made with exactness.

The second detail we should take from this is the description of Christ with all His angels. In the accounts of the lives of some saints we read of how an encounter with just a single angel is terrifying and awe-inspiring. The sight of the whole host of angels with Christ in His glory will be a terrible and unimaginable moment that will shatter every pretence and vain source of pride. As Christ appears as Judge there will be an instant and solemn awareness in men of the evil they have chosen and a great mourning will occur amongst those who have united themselves with Satan even if it has been done unknowingly. The Final Judgement will be just that, a final and eternal determining of who we are, about which we have had numerous warnings. As Saint Cyprian of Carthage writes:

Too late will they believe in eternal punishment those who would not believe in eternal life.

In Matthew's Gospel Christ's description continues with Him casting the unrighteous into Gehenna, a Jewish image taken from the valley outside Jerusalem where refuge and filth was thrown from the city. Here and again in the Book of Revelation we are told it is like a lake of fire that burns eternally. This terrible end is the seriousness with which Christ wants us to engage with the appalling state of those who reject God. It is defilement at its very worse because it is in direct conflict with the purpose and nature of our existence. Created to be in union with God man would cast that union aside in favour of delusions and self-glorification. The terrible realisation of what has been rejected will be more painful than any fire, and the incompatibility between the purity of God and a blackened soul will be the true barrier that prevents the unrighteous from joining the blessed. God's infinite mercy and love seeks out every man while he lives, we must not apply anthropomorphic ideas of human anger to God. Every man is blessed by God, but only in uniting ourselves to Christ and being transformed into His likeness can we receive these blessings.

Concerning God's judgement there have been speculations about who will be saved and what proportion of humanity will enter Heaven. Universalists have maintained that a loving God could not permit any to be lost but this runs contrary to the warnings of Christ and from other parts of scripture. *Few will enter,* we are warned, for the *gate is narrow*. Until the hour arrives we cannot know these things, our concern therefore should be to ensure that we focus on those things for which we are responsible: our salvation and the salvation of those whom God as entrusted to us. While visiting Mount Athos I discussed this issue with a monk who expressed the belief that anyone who cries out to God before the Final Judgement will be saved. He explained that this was compatible with Christ's teaching but that it did not assume that everyone who cried out would be rewarded in equal measure. The Church teaches that according to the degree of holiness which we have acquired on earth so our place before God will be different. We will each be able to stand different levels of God's glory: the holiest of saints will be nearer to Him than most of us. This is a comforting thought for those who have lost loved ones and worry that their departed did not appear to be united to God. Who amongst us can categorically explain any other man's heart? God alone knows the secrets within us and we must have hope that perhaps even at the hour of death our loved ones cried out to him in their soul. This is why the manner of our death is so important, because as the process of biological death brings us closer to the spiritual world we may be given the opportunity to cry out one last time, like the thief who was crucified beside Christ.

The New Testament describes Christ standing before the unlawful San Hedrin (unlawful because the Law of Moses prescribed one High Priest at any time and Jesus was brought before a group of them). This corrupt group of Jews conspired to murder their King to protect their worldly interests and because their hearts were far from the truth recognised even by simple fishermen. They misinterpreted the Law in order to kill the One Who gave the Law, such was the evil they had embraced. The evil council called witnesses to give false testimony against Him, but at the final Judgement no witnesses or papers will be necessary: the book will be opened which is the soul within us revealing good or evil. In the middle of the night they took Him in secret, their judgement came from Satan and the shadows. This picture is the exact opposite of how we shall be judged. Christ's light will illuminate the shadows where our corruption is hidden, He will come openly for all to see, and the condemned will know the justice they have brought down upon themselves. Let us try to show mercy to one another, to forgive even as we hope to be forgiven. How can we call out for compassion if we have withheld it from our neighbour? In the Lord's Prayer we say *Forgive us our sins as we forgive those who sin against us*. How often we have said this to God, but who amongst us would be willing right now to be judged by Almighty God according to the measure of mercy we have really shown others? Let us grieve with the widow and welcome the stranger, for in our hour of grief at the Final Judgement God will see the true measure of our forgiveness. Let us imitate Christ Who forgave His persecutors and not copy those who are mad with power and devour one another for the sake of a coin or piece of bread. When others injure us let us learn to pray for the injury they really commit against themselves, counting our own needs and hurts as nothing.

Let us now consider how we should know that these things are coming to pass. In general terms Christ said to look for wars, earthquakes, famine, strife and confusion. We might wonder if there was ever any time when men couldn't look at the world around them and see such things occurring. But we live in days with more specific signs that may be observed. We are told to watch for a falling away of faith, a lack of morality and denial of God's law when men will become proud. Since the age of enlightenment there has been a growing sense of man's ingenuity which has only increased with the rapid change in technology over recent years. Men marvel at the signs and wonders of science, they conform their thinking to theories about the nature of existence that deny God, in short the spirit of this age is rapidly moving towards evil. New forms of moral thinking are espoused and traditional values mocked and then deemed evil: a teacher in a British state school would lose his job if he told a class of students that he believed that same sex marriage is a sin. We should not be surprised by this since the book of Revelation tells us that in the last days the Church will hide away in the wilderness, unable to show herself in public. The world is corrupting us and turning us against Christ. What is good will be slandered as evil. The world breaks us down step by step, layer by layer, normalising sin and immorality in order to eventually draw men into rejecting God. Television hypnotises and misguides the unwary; children are left to the attack of demons without any spiritual protection. The signs of our times are growing, we see the State of Israel slaughtering countless children in Palestine as thoughts turn to the rebuilding of the Temple: when this is accomplished the time is very near for the Anti-Christ will claim himself to be God in that very place. As Saint John Maxamovitch tells us,

The Anti-Christ will choose Jerusalem as his capital, because it was here that the Saviour revealed His Divine teaching and His person, and the whole world was called to the blessedness of goodness and salvation. But the world did not accept Christ and crucified Him in Jerusalem: while under Anti-Christ, Jerusalem will become the capital of the world that has recognised the authority of Anti-Christ.

Only when men have rejected the truth will they believe in deception, and we are already at a time when men will believe almost anything except the truth. We must look for the movement to a single world government that will enable demonic rule to be accomplished, we should watch carefully in matters of economics and politics to see how it is being accomplished. None of us knows the hour, but Christ calls us to watch for the signs that we may have the courage to endure and remain faithful. As long as we know how the tribulations will end we can pray that God will sustain us until Christ's return. But above all we must repent and live inwardly in such a way that when our hearts, our thoughts and our actions, are laid out before us we may not be ashamed but may dance with joy at Christ's coming.

Heaven And Hell

We now turn our focus to a topic that has become quite confused in the minds of many people in the West: Heaven and Hell. The medieval West saw many myths and false ideas entering the general perception of what the Church teaches about Heaven and Hell. Some of this was as a result of artistic interpretation that became established in people's minds as reality and other misconceptions were a result of the Roman Catholic use of reward and punishment in order to get people to do what they wanted (for example take part in crusades). Let us first identify what the Church teaches as dogma before turning to other ideas.

The Church has established in scripture and tradition that we know the condition of the saints in Heaven. First we are taught that they have eternal rest from labours, that there is no demand placed on them to earn their reward. Second we are assured that they do not experience any kind of grief, sorrow or pain, they are free from every kind of suffering. Third we see that they share in a form of mutual communion that exceeds anything on earth and that this is enjoyed between people and angels. The fourth feature is that the blessed stand before the Throne of God and see Him face to face as they serve Him. They have a direct and immediate contact with God that is beyond anything known on earth. Finally we believe that the saints are not present with Christ as subjects, but as adopted heirs and reign with Him.

Concerning Hell we must guard ourselves against the themes of medieval doom paintings intended to frighten people into obedience to the Roman Church. It is clear from scripture that the eternal fire is prepared for the devil and his demons (Matthew 5) and not for humanity. The false idea that the devil rules over a kingdom in Hell where poor souls go to be tortured by him is not Christian teaching and creates a disturbing image of God. While Heaven is prepared for those who repent, the unrepentant demons must be separated from eternal Paradise and will be cast out at the Final Judgement.

A key moment in our understanding comes from the New Testament when Jesus promises the thief that he will be in Paradise with Him. The thief had previously asked *remember me in your Kingdom.* Christ's Kingdom is Paradise. Those who are obedient to God enter the Kingdom of God. In Jewish thinking the Kingdom was not described like a place but as the reign of God: where God reigns there is His Kingdom. Paradise is therefore the state of utter obedience to the perfect and loving will of God.

Therefore it is not helpful to see Heaven and Hell as being two different geographical places, as portrayed in medieval art, but as two forms of existence or states of being. They are in fact the consequences of different internal states in response to God's love. At Judgement this love is revealed in Christ in all His majesty and divinity: only hearts that are repentant and transformed by God's Holy Spirit can see Christ as Paradise. The eternal state of humanity is really the same single reality; Heaven and Hell are the different experiences of the same presence of God. This is why we repeatedly read in the Church Fathers of God being the unending fire; Saint John of the Ladder describes Christ's presence as *an all-consuming fire and an illuminating light* while Saint Gregory Palamas explains:

Thus it is said, He will baptise you by the Holy Spirit and by fire: in other words by illumination and punishment, depending on each person's predisposition, which will bring upon him that which he deserves.

This is an important point to make because it distinguishes the Church's teaching from popular ideas of God condemning people to Hell. The idea in Calvinism that God deliberately creates some men for damnation is abhorrent and must be rejected if we are to be able to approach God as He really is. We should move away from the conception of Hell as divine retribution, God's love is poured out to each of us equally, but we determine our own ability to receive it. If we reject love through out our lives and fail to repent then

134

we form a soul within us that is unable to stand the sight of Christ, His uncreated light will be to us no less than Hell. Of course God is also just, and we must not take His love as an assurance that we will not be held accountable for actions.

This understanding of Heaven and Hell sits at the very heart of the difference between Orthodoxy and the various heretical Christian groups that have appeared in recent centuries. While they, like so many pagan religions, seek an eternal state of bliss as a reward, it is the restoration, healing and attainment of *theosis* that the Orthodox must work for. It is for this reason that God created us, *to find a place in the majesty of the divine kingdom* as Saint Gregory Palamas writes.

If this is the glorious purpose for which we are created, we must wonder why there are some of us who choose not to accept it. For love to be real we have identified that it cannot be forced, there must be an act of free will or else it is not love. We are endowed with the capacity to love, but equally with the choice to reject love and choose evil. But God does not reject us when we do this; it is we who are rejecting God in such choices. Therefore it must be recognised that the fiery torments alluded to earlier were never intended for us but for the demons, however, we can choose to join them if we wish.

This teaching is exactly what we see in the parable of Lazarus and the rich man, for both men having died look at the same God, but one with consolation the other with anguish. Like the rich man we have all been given the option to love or live selfishly. In the parable Christ says that the rich man when he died went down into the dust. In truth he had already buried himself in the things of the earth long before his death. This is the choice we are all faced with, whether to pursue the material pleasures that satisfy us or to perceive the needs of others around us. The parable of the sheep and the goats, where Christ divides humanity according to how we have cared for others is indicative of this internal state: our outward actions are the signs of the change within. Theosis is not a process that drives us into isolated spiritual states but transforms the way we treat other people: visiting the sick, the prisoner and the widow reveal that we have God within us.

A further Roman Catholic heresy is the idea of *the absence of God*. This maintains that those in Hell will not be able to see God. Certainly the unrepentant soul will sense his loss of God in a shameful realisation that he has made himself unable to bear God's presence, but this is not the same as God casting someone out from himself, it is a sense of separation that begins with us not God. It is a consequence of the idea that Hell is God's punishment and so is a place of rejection where man is cast away. Orthodoxy refutes this myth, teaching that no one will ever be beyond God's presence for He is in all things and everywhere present. The heresy is also a result of the false idea that Heaven and Hell are separate spaces in geographical terms which has found its way into western culture as a result of fiction such as Dante's Inferno. But what is recognised in common is that the condition of Heaven or Hell is a final stage, there is no movement from one to the other. The eternal movement of the saved towards greater knowledge of God is not a movement from Hell to Heaven. This final reality is a sobering prospect which should encourage us all to make the most of the time God has given us in this life, not as a threat that hangs over us but as a reminder that this earthly period of existence has immense purpose and value. The pleasures of this world will be our damnation if we make them the goal of our lives, just like the rich man in the parable. We are mistaken if we see this as some kind of divine threat; it is the caring guidance of a Father Who wants to protect us from ourselves. The laws of God are not an arbitrary set of rules but the way he sets out the path to Heaven before us: He even came and walked that path with us so that we might see clearly where to tread. Anyone who tries to hold God accountable for those who enter Hell has failed to recognise that the responsibility is entirely our own: each of us accepts or rejects salvation. The burning bush witnessed by Moses is a reminder that the coming of God burns without destruction, so that the soul which has rejected love does not burn into nothingness, it experiences the presence of God as an unwanted fire for all eternity. This is why the psalmist tells us that fear of God teaches wisdom: for spiritual infancy it is necessary but we must move beyond this. The high value placed on man in Orthodox theology is such that he is called to become a "little god" by Grace (not in essence like God Himself). But this high esteem means that we recognise that in all things God has given us the role of collaboration. Divine Grace does not obliterate our will; God continuously calls us to work with Him in the process of our redemption. The healing required within us can only take place with our active co-operation, it is by both Grace and works that man is saved. When we understand this we engage with the great dignity of what it is to be human, that the Creator of all things should trust us with such a precious commodity as an eternal soul. To be eternally present in the love of God is to be eternally loved by Him, with a love that is infinite and perfect. This great love permits us the responsibility to choose the eternal condition of that which is loved so much by Him. Every parent knows the trust involved when leaving their child in the care of others: God has trusted us as communities and families with the nurture of one another, giving us everything necessary to travel together along the narrow path. Even our own soul is loved more by God than we can love ourselves, He entrusts us with our own lives. While the devil speaks through men blinded by materialism and tries to convince us that Hell is not real, Christ warns us of its torments: the one who wishes to drag us there pretends that it doesn't exist while the One Who came to save us from it is portrayed by the devil as severe because He speaks openly about its dangers.

The greatest means of finding God's Grace is through the sacramental life of the Church. The Kingdom of God enters us each time we receive Holy Communion. Christ is the way, the life and the truth, to receive Him physically into our bodies is to unite ourselves with the spiritual Kingdom of Heaven. The transformation of our inner being is not achieved simply through great effort, though this effort is required, it is God's Grace that makes such effort possible. But just as the experience of God at judgement will be either as Heaven or Hell, so too our meeting with Him at the Eucharist can be either as salvation or condemnation. Before Holy Communion is distributed the priest always prays that we may receive Him *not unto condemnation and judgement but unto eternal life*. It is our meeting with Christ at the Eucharist that prepares us for our meeting with Him at judgement. This is why it is so important that we reflect and repent before receiving Holy Communion, and why in some parts of the Church the tradition is to make confession before receiving. In the same way we should try to see every part of our life as a preparation for that final meeting, so that everything becomes part of the process of our redemption. Saint Basil expresses this concisely when he says:

Those things therefore that lead us towards that life, should be cherished and pursued with all our might; and those that do not lead us there, we should disregard, as something of no value.

Many Protestant groups have become so concerned with outreach and mission that they have lost sight of the true purpose of Christianity which is the preparation of our souls for eternity. If we truly participate in the life of God then faith will always produce good works: without them it is dead. But how ironic that so many groups that profess that salvation is the result of faith without works have become fixated with social work and fail to give the necessary attention that faith and the soul need. The Church is not a ship onto which we leap once and for all and then sit back while it carries us to Paradise. The Kingdom of Heaven must grow within us, it requires that we keep on rowing; we must attend to the sails, bail out water from the hull, and trust in the One Who charts our course through dangerous seas.

Purgatory

The next two chapters are concerned with false beliefs relating to death. It is important to believe the truth to avoid false ideas about God but also to protect us from the consequences of these beliefs both in terms of our thinking and behaviour. There is one further reason why we should understand and believe the truth and that is because it is an issue of morality. While western culture emphasises individualism and following what feels right to us personally, the Early Church was clear that right belief is as much a moral issue as right action. If we choose to believe heresy we are being immoral just as if we were stealing or committing adultery. In fact many saints identified false belief as far more destructive and serious than immoral actions, and there are few subjects where it is more important to avoid heresy than death, judgement and resurrection. We shall first look at the idea of purgatory and in the following chapter consider a number of other false ideas that confuse people's thinking.

In one sense it could be argued that the development of the idea of purgatory was an expression of the western church's desire to see all men saved: a reasonable desire in itself. Recognising that many people die in a deeply sinful state the intention was to create a means of explaining how such sinners could be changed after death to a state that would make them acceptable for Heaven.

The Roman teaching about purgatory was not officially declared until the year 1274 at the Council of Lyons (it is important that we recognise that this was two hundred and twenty years after the schism that separated Rome from the Church, this was not an Ecumenical Council and does not have any authority). The doctrine proposed that there is a specific place in which the dead are sent to suffer punishments for the sins they have committed and so atone for them. This atonement is recognised as being for all the sins a person has committed, whether they have repented or not. For Rome the act of repentance was not seen as sufficient to cleanse a person and so they maintained that we must, in addition, suffer in this life proportionally to our sins. It was an idea later developed at the Roman Council of Florence in 1439. The teaching was immediately condemned by the Orthodox, for example Saint Mark, Bishop of Ephesus acknowledged that God cleanses us from our sin but *not by means of some purgatorial fire or a definite punishment in some place.* Saint Mark stated the faith handed down from the Apostles which teaches that the purification that God completes of the saints before their entry into Heaven in no way involves punishment. The notion of such punishment is an affront to faith in a loving

God and sits in contradiction to the faith in all that is accomplished by Christ's death and resurrection.

While we may want to be generous in applying loving reasons to the development of this heresy, the Roman church's further developments must be condemned without any effort to attribute positive motives. After the Council of Florence Rome taught that those with sufficient wealth could purchase indulgences which would enable their dead to escape the necessary suffering to purify their soul. Some payments could completely remove the required punishment while others would simply reduce it. Rome concluded that such indulgences were possible because of the extra merits of the saints in Heaven who had earned more merit than was necessary for their own salvation and which could be applied to others. Of course, during periods of Roman expansion such payment enabled the building of impressive churches and Rome was able to establish itself as a powerful earthly presence amongst the jostling kingdoms and empires of men.

Having frightened people with the blasphemous idea of God punishing the unworthy, they then offered the rich the opportunity to buy God off. As for the dead of the poor in purgatory we can only assume that their families' poverty must be an offence to God if He is unwilling to alleviate their suffering like that of the rich!

The Orthodox teaching has always been that nothing can merit salvation except the Grace of God. Although we can even see elements of these false ideas in Augustine's writings we must rightly reject them. The rejection of the foolishness of indulgences was one of the causes of the movement that led to the Reformation, but sadly in rejecting this heresy they also rejected the truths on which it was based: the intercession of the saints and the communion of the Church on earth and in Heaven.

There are, however, certain subtleties to this issue that need to be examined in more detail. Some Orthodox thinkers do consider there to be a form of purification after death, echoing those Orthodox who agreed with declarations from the Council of Florence. In particular there are some who teach that though we may have repented in this life, the true fruits of repentance are not always forthcoming in our lives, but they do not agree with this resulting in purgatorial fire. Even saint Mark of Ephesus acknowledged that:

The souls of those who depart this life with true repentance and in the love of God before they have rendered satisfaction for their trespasses and negligences by worthy fruits of repentance, are cleansed after death by cleansing pains.

While some Roman theologians have tried to interpret this as being in agreement over purgatory, being a matter of replacing the word *fire* with *pains*, when we look at the broader meaning of his statements we find categorically the rejection of such pains being in a designated place of suffering. Having been impressed by many Roman speakers, the Orthodox declared their rejection after the Council, in large part to Saint Mark's holy words.

A further level of complication over this matter occurred when the Orthodox had to deal with the innovations espoused in the west by the Reformation writers. A Synod was called in 1672 which produced what is called "The Confession of Dositheus". This was presented to defend the Apostolic faith, and in it the bishops pronounced that the soul goes to an immediate state which is a limited foretaste of Heaven or Hell until the General Resurrection. This is an important point because it makes clear that our prayers for the dead can have an effect, since the final and complete conditions of Heaven and Hell have not yet been entered, but at the same time it in no way permits the teaching of a place for purgatory.

It could be argued that the heresy of purgatory is more akin to pagan ideas about reincarnation than it is to authentic Christian teaching. Both the beliefs in multiple lives and in the idea that we must suffer in an appointed place are based on the notion of us purified by something other than Grace. Theosis is a very different belief since it maintains that we co-operate with God's Grace, but we do not replace it with something else, we work to enable ourselves to be changed by God's Grace.

Who amongst us finds peace in the notion that God burns our loved ones in this way? There is no biblical foundation for the doctrine of purgatory, and the main early exponent of the idea, Origen, was condemned for it at the Fifth Ecumenical Council. The belief does not stand up to inspection since it fails to reflect the full Christian view of man and salvation. Since we believe that we will be resurrected in both body and soul, the idea that punishment of the soul is sufficient to save them both is illogical and goes against the nature of Christ's own suffering in both body and soul.

The belief in purgatory is also dangerous because it gives a false sense of unimportance to our repentance in this life. If we are able to rely on a time of punishment that will cleanse us of our sins, why should we really worry for now? The truth is we must repent in this life for when we are dead it will be too late. The devil would have us put off what is necessary for salvation to some later date and so much the better if we would leave it until after death. Purgatory denies both the necessity for repentance and the power given by Christ to the Church to forgive sins. When we receive absolution after confessing our sins we must believe in the reality of that sacrament, or else we are playing games and fooling ourselves.

Purgatory returns to that belief in Christ's death as a penal substitution since it maintains that in order to enter Heaven God must be satisfied that sufficient punishment has been dealt out. It insists that God feels anger towards us and that His justice must be satisfied. But who could believe that any suffering we endure could ever be sufficient to make us worthy of Heaven? If this were the case there would have been no need for the incarnation of Christ, no need for His death and resurrection. We could each have been given sufficient pain in purgatory to cleanse us of our sin. Such blasphemy denies the infinite and priceless sacrifice that Christ has made for us.

While we have stressed the therapeutic nature of the sacraments and the whole life of the Church, to suddenly fall back into a belief that we must be punished sits in direct opposition to such faith. Salvation is about healing and restoration, not punishment. As was stated at the beginning of this chapter, false belief corrupts our whole relationship with God. If we accept the Roman concept of a God that punishes our loved ones and will do so to us, we have a strange idea of what a loving Father is like. God's love and mercy is not expressed in the punishment of purgatory, we must not allow ourselves to be unsettled by such heresy. This life on earth is the time in which God will make us fit for Heaven. The Kingdom of God is within us, let us manifest it in repentance and acts of love.

✠

The Rapture and Other Heresies

The prospect of our death or the death of those we love can leave us confused and vulnerable, not least to ideas that might seem appealing or comforting. It is important that we establish ourselves in the truth before we find ourselves in the emotional intensity of bereavement. In some ways false ideas that are very different from authentic Christianity are less dangerous because they are more alien to us and easier to recognise for what they are. Heresies wrapped in biblical quotations and delivered by those masquerading as the Church can mislead the unwary. This chapter is concerned with some of these false beliefs, first dealing with reincarnation and chiliasm before looking carefully at the belief known as the rapture.

In Buddhism and Hinduism it is taught that we have many lives in which we must slowly work our way towards an ultimate goal: for Hindus this is moksha, for Buddhists it is the state of enlightenment and nirvana. Although the two systems proclaim reincarnation, they have very different understandings of what it means.

The most common understanding of reincarnation amongst westerners comes from Hinduism. Hindus believe that the atman (soul) moves from one incarnation to the next as it works towards release from rebirth so that it can become one with the divine source of being. Buddhism is different in that it denies that there is a God or even a permanent self that is identifiable as a continuous person, but like in Hinduism maintains that the person struggles through many lives to lose all desire and so reach enlightenment. In this way the two systems convince adherents that nothing is final in this life, that there is always more time in another life to achieve what must be done. For Buddhists the focus is entirely on the individual's will, the achievement of nirvana is down to us and no one else. While many westerners are attracted to a belief system that promises inner peace without resort to God, their rejection of Christ in this way leaves them vulnerable to demonic attack and delusion.

The two systems of belief teach that access to this process of change comes through meditation. There are various traditions and forms of meditation in both religions, including repetition of mantras and breathing exercises. While it is certainly true that modern man needs more than ever to make time to find quiet and free himself from distraction and that there may be psychological effects from sitting in silence, Christianity maintains that the focus at such times must be on the presence of God if it is to have spiritual benefit. The mind can be rested from its anxieties through many things, including exercise and pharmaceuticals, and though this may make us feel happier in the short term, it does not lead to eternal peace. Everything we do in this world directs towards or away from redemption, we must not seek elevated states of mind as a reward in themselves: the demons can prompt such feelings. Spiritual sensuality is worse than physical sensuality, both are a craving for experience, but delighting our soul with false satisfaction prevents it from craving its true purpose.

A more insidious heresy is that of chiliasm which teaches that Christ will return and reign on earth for a thousand years (named from the Greek for a thousand years, *chiliasmos*). Rather than there being a General Resurrection of all the dead chiliasm claims that only the righteous will rise to reign with Christ. Only after they have enjoyed a thousand years on earth together will the unrighteous be raised and judged.

The error is in the interpretation of the twentieth chapter of the Book of Revelation which speaks of the first resurrection: chiliasts take this to be a literal event while the early Church knew it to refer to spiritual rebirth through baptism. The spread of this belief required its formal rejection when the Church declared it a heresy at the Second Ecumenical Council. This is why Christians repeat at near the end of the Creed the words *And His Kingdom will have no end*, to declare the rejection of a thousand year reign that will come to an end.

Let us turn now to the *rapture* which has found acceptance amongst so many Protestant groups in the United States of America. We could be forgiven for thinking that the rapture is a reformation idea since it is so prevalent amongst Protestants, but in fact it does not appear in the writings of Luther, Calvin or the Wesley brothers. Today it is still alien to the Anglicans and Methodists who attempt to maintain a modicum of connection with the traditional teachings of the Church, so we should begin by asking where it came from.

It is at the end of the nineteenth century that we first see reference to the term *the rapture* in the sermons and writings of John Nelson Darby, an Irish evangelist at work in America. The heresy caught on amongst evangelicals and was given a good deal of publicity by the writer William Blackstone. Although the theory started amongst Darby's Plymouth Brethren it has today gained acceptance amongst Baptists, Pentecostalists and other fundamentalist groups through a number of sources. Various writers in the nineteen sixties and seventies popularised it as a response to perceptions about ecological disaster, and in the last twenty years there have been a growing number of works of fiction, both published and cinematic, which use the theme of the rapture as the basis of their plots.

The United States has always been a fruitful ground for sects and heretical groups, particularly those which claimed special insight into when Christ would return. A number of Seventh Day

Adventists for example have made a series of claims about dates on which the Second Coming would occur. As these dates drew near and then passed by without incident, the groups simply reinterpreted their messages and looked forward to the next date.

Believers in the rapture await a cataclysmic event when millions of people will disappear, they will be the righteous who will be taken up into Heaven before the time of tribulation occurs when great disasters and suffering befalls those who are left behind. Its attraction to Americans is not hard to understand. In a culture where too often individual success is considered a sign of blessing, and expensive cars fill mega-church car parks in testimony to how righteous the occupants are, the notion of poverty and suffering is mistaken for a lack of faith or righteousness. With such a mindset, the kinds of travails Saint John describes in the Book of Revelation must surely be meant for someone other than God's elect! Belief in the rapture is really the desire to avoid suffering, it is a belief that God will help us to escape before it gets too bad. In fact the Church has always taught that these sufferings will befall the Body of Christ, just as His body was scourged and tormented during the incarnation. The modern desire for ease and comfort is in direct opposition to the aesthetic nature of Christianity, and the enthusiastic willingness to believe in the rapture only demonstrates how far so many Protestant groups have moved from the truth. But Christians who genuinely seek God must ask themselves why this teaching never appeared in the Early Church, in the Reformation, or at any time in history until modern times. How could God withhold such revelation from all the prophets, Apostles, saints and martyrs of the Church only to reveal this *new teaching* in America in our times? Christ did not promise to remove His Church from the hour of trial, He prayed:

I do not pray that you should take them out of the world but that you should keep them from the evil one (John 17[15]).

The Church recognises that the elect will suffer in the days before Christ's return for Satan will turn his full fury on the followers of Christ. We are assured by Christ that the time will be kept mercifully short so that we may not lose heart: He at no point promises to lift us from the earth to avoid the suffering. It is an evil deception that assures us that we need not prepare ourselves for the time ahead. The danger of the rapture is its assurance that the love we know God has for us will prevent us from being tested. Satan wants the Church unprepared, the Church of the catacombs did not wonder why God had not whisked them away, but endured because it remembered Christ's words that what the world did to Him it would do to those who followed Him.

When we reflect on the power of the image of Christ's Second Coming we cannot accept that He will return in secret to take up to Heaven the elect seven years before His final coming. In the words of the Creed we declare that *He will come again in glory*. It is an event for which we must prepare our hearts; we must be steadfast and expect no better treatment than Christ received Himself. Countless saints have given their lives for the Gospel: if we are to be citizens of Heaven we must be prepared to be renounced by this world.

Angels

There are many false ideas that have developed about angels, partly due to folk religion and partly due to fictional portrayals that have entered our cultural consciousness and somehow replaced the truth. Many people reject the existence of angels because they have been exposed to sentimental ideas which have no similarity to reality. From my own childhood I can recount many examples where the idea was presented that when someone dies they become an angel: it is a heresy that runs from Tom and Jerry cartoons (where the cat was often killed and then seen rising with wings and a harp) to multi-million dollar movies. But these silly ideas only conceal the nature and purpose of angels and can prevent people seeking the help that angels offer. In this chapter we will consider the role of angels with regards to our passage from this world, we will examine the angel of death and also make clear the Church's teaching about our Guardian Angels (a subject that has been thoroughly misunderstood because of romantic fantasies).

The word *angel* means messenger and one of the key roles they have is to reveal God's will to mankind. The existence of angels was made known to man from the very beginning and when he was cast out of Paradise it was an angel which stood guarding the entry through the gates of Eden. They appear many times in the Old and New Testaments, most importantly to announce to the Holy Virgin Mary that she was going to conceive God's Son. Shepherds witnessed them rejoicing at Christ's birth and at Christ's resurrection the myrrh-bearing women were informed by an angel that their Lord was alive.

The invisible world was created by God along with the visible one, and many Church Fathers suggest that the heavens were made much earlier than this world. The angels have free will and reason; they serve God and are only made visible to us when God wills it. Since they are incorporeal spirits they can travel to any point in the universe in an instant but when they are in Heaven they are not on earth, and when on earth they are not in Heaven: they are not omni-present as God is. Angels have been granted immortality through God's Grace just as humans have, and so they can never die. The Church teaches that angels are capable of great heights of spiritual development and have intellectual capacities far in excess of that of humans, but they do not know the future and cannot perform miracles except through the will and power of God. The number of angels is vast, many biblical references identify rank upon rank and thousands upon thousands of them, their number is many times greater than all the people who have or ever will live. Some angels are identified as archangels and so we understand that they are organised by rank and position within a hierarchy before God. The closest rank to God is the cherubim and seraphim, then come the authorities, dominion and powers and finally the principalities, angels and archangels which interact with us. Various references are made in the Bible to nine specific ranks (though some Church fathers maintain that these are only the ones revealed to us in this age with far more yet to be known); indicating that the heavenly realm is ordered and that there are levels of existence signifying degrees of perfection and nearness to God.

Angels reflect God's glory and sing hymns before His throne. Their worship is the reason Orthodox worship is intended to be as beautiful as possible: our human activity joins with and reflects angelic worship. Angels have responsibility and connection with different aspects of the created order including human beings. We are each assigned a Guardian Angel to watch over us and pray for us who remains with us through out our life (unless we live in such an evil way that we drive them away from us). Saint Ambrose writes: *pray to your angels, who are given to us as guardians.* This is echoed in the words of Saint Jerome who tells us:

So great is the dignity of soul that each man has, from the beginning of his birth, been given an angel who is designated to guard him.

And again, Clement of Alexandria writes: *Regiments of angels are distributed over nations*

157

and cities, and some are assigned to particular individuals.

In fact Guardian Angles were known of by the Jews (Psalm 34) and Christ refers to them when He says:

Take heed that you do not despise one of these little ones, for I say unto you that in Heaven their angels always see the face of my Father Who is in Heaven (Matthew 18[10]).

We are to pray for help from our angels and also seek their intercessions as we do those of the saints. Becoming aware of our angelic companion through life can give great courage and also comfort, and when we are concerned for the well being of our family and friends we should pray to their Guardian Angels that they will watch over them. A friend who is a priest working in a secondary school confided that when confronted with very unruly classes of children he will often pray to their angels with noticeable results.

Before looking specifically at the connection between angels and the subject of death we must acknowledge the existence of those angels that have been cast out of Heaven. The demons were once angels in Heaven and possess all of the intelligence and speed attributed earlier to the other angels. This makes them a formidable enemy to mankind: an enemy we could not possibly hope to defeat without God's help. The demons wish to cause as much confusion amongst mankind as possible, especially about death and judgement. Their impersonation of the dead at spiritualist meetings is just one example and they have been described as appearing like angels of light to mislead the unwary. This is why the Church always directs us to refuse any angelic visitation: if it is genuine then God will forgive us. Their acute intellect and ability to travel great distances in a moment affords them the capacity to reveal things as though predicting the future and so convincing us that they are sent by God.

Satan was created as a beautiful angel called Lucifer (which means light-bearer) but chose to disobey God through pride, loving his own appearance as though it were his beyond God's gift. This sense of his own beauty and greatness is the root of so much of our sin too, so many of our actions are ultimately motivated by pride. Whenever we do anything to our own glory we are following the path Satan first walked: and in our ear we may have the flattery of demons encouraging us to follow it. When pride has completely overcome us then even the notion of repentance becomes abhorrent which is the condition of those for whom God's presence will be hell. Saint Irenaeus tells us:

The devil, since he is an apostate angel, is able to lead astray and to deceive the mind of man for the transgressing of God's commands. Little by little he can darken the hearts of men – to the point that forgetting the true God, they adore the devil as if he were true God.

Tertullian warns more bluntly: *The business of the fallen angels, who are the demons, is to corrupt mankind.* This is why great care and awareness is necessary; we must always be on our guard against the prowling lion. We must learn to recognise the truth of our feelings and emotions, begin to see our real goals and purposes so that we can root out through repentance the corruption of pride and ego.

The tradition of the Church tells us that when the Theotokos was praying on the Mount of Olives, where Jesus had ascended to Heaven, the angel Gabriel appeared to her and assured her that her wish to be with her son would soon be granted. The angel assured her that bodily death would have no power over her soul and she knew no fear of what would happen to her. Many saints have assured us that angels will attend to us at our death, and that our passage from this life to the next will be easier if we strengthen the bond with our Guardian Angel in this world. If we come to know and have a spiritual intimacy with our angelic protector then we will naturally turn to them when we die.

The figure of the Angel of Death (often wearing black and carrying a scythe to cut us down at the appointed hour) is found in the Jewish Talmud as an evil being who God permits to visit unrighteous people (righteous Jews are assured that it will stay away from them). It is an unpleasant image (typical of the Talmud which was heavily influenced by Babylonian paganism). Muslims too believe in a figure who comes for us when God decides it is our time to die. In Christian tradition, however, there is no such single angel appointed to carry out such missions. Since death is made into a holy event by Christ's death and resurrection, there is no evil angel needed at the time of death for this work, however, as we have seen in our examination of what happens to the soul after death, there are certainly both angels and demons around the soul at that time. But this should not be taken as a reason to become fretful since we live in a world where angels and demons are at work every day. If we wish to remain protected from their influence we should seek the path of trying to love God and our neighbour as our self.

The reality of the angels is difficult to accept for minds deeply immersed in the material world, their presence is only understood when we are alive to God and the spiritual nature of existence. When someone has lived without a sense of angelic support death will be difficult for them because they will not be accustomed to finding the help they need when the body dies. Prayer and awareness of the angelic forces in the world helps to ready us for what is to come; they train our focus and sensitivity to the true nature of being. When we begin to live prayerfully we enter that realm where we will be after death and similarly we begin to leave this one even while still in the body. If we do not draw closer to God in this life and allow Him to transform us then the shock of death will be disastrous for us. Preparation for that event must happen now while God grants us time to do so, we must accept the help of His angels and live as those ready to depart.

Martyrdom

The right view of death is best understood when we consider the martyrs of the Church. In a world where so much time and effort is spent prolonging life the martyrs teach us how to recognise the true value of faith and help us to gain a healthy perspective on our death. Many martyrs did not simply face death but also terrible tortures and humiliations before they were killed. Their blood is witness to the peace that God can give us and how faith can enable us to become conquerors with Christ. Saint Paul tells us bluntly that *All who desire to live godly in Christ Jesus will suffer persecution* (2 Timothy 3^{12}).

From the very beginning of the Church's existence there have been persecutions of those who follow Christ. The very first to give his earthly life for Christ was Saint Stephen who was stoned to death by a Jewish mob intent on wiping out the emerging Church. His death is more powerful than any teaching in words; it conveys something profound and inspiring. The same sacrificial love we see in Christ is at work in the martyrs who offer themselves to God without holding anything back. It is an utter abandonment to His love, a recognition that not even life itself is to be considered as anything of importance compared to union with Him. The meaning of the

163

cross is made plain in martyrdom; the victory that Christ established over death transforms each of our deaths and martyrdom is the most powerful sign of faith in this truth. The history of the Church has seen persistent waves of persecution, each a kind of foretaste of the bitter suffering that will engulf the world before Christ's final return. Christians should note that just as the first followers of Christ found themselves to be a small group in the midst of a pagan culture so increasingly the Church in the West finds itself at odds with the prevailing attitudes and beliefs that surround it. The Church must never chase the approval of the world.

Martyrdom reminds us of the brevity of life in this world and that we can only find meaning in this reality when we are confident of eternal life. Such confidence must make us see ourselves as those merely passing through as strangers, we are those who journey to our true home and we must see this life as preparation. As Saint Paul writes:

While we are at home in the body we are absent from the Lord; for we walk in faith not by sight. We are confident, I say, and willing rather to be absent from the body and to be present with the Lord (2 Corinthians 5[6-8]).

If we are to declare this to the world then there must be martyrs or else the world will know that the faith we speak of is not real. The word *martyr* is derived from the word *witness* and was originally used in reference to the Apostles as they witnessed to the truth of Christ. Tertullian observed that the more severe the torture the more people were converted by the courage of the martyrs, he noticed that the number of Christians grew during persecution while the number of those who carried out the persecution dwindled. Each time we suffer persecution for Christ we are witnesses, and so martyrdom does not always require the shedding of our blood. But every form of martyrdom requires forbearance and faith, and we will not be ready to face death for Christ if we do not practise bloodless martyrdom each time we are accused or suffer injustice. Similarly the ascetic rules of the Church about fasting help us to deny our body's desires and help teach us discipline. As Saint Isaac the Syrian writes:

Ease and idleness are the destruction of the soul and they can injure her more than demons.

Martyrdom has involved many forms of torture and ill treatment. Christians have been robbed of their social or legal rights, they have suffered insults and mocking, they have been tortured for months and even years and many female Christians have endured appalling sexual violence. If we allow ourselves to imagine this world and this life as the sum of our existence then we will feel every blow as having importance and relevance. But seeing ourselves as brief sojourners here helps us to recognise the petty nature of harsh words spoken against us or even the pains of death. Seeing this converted many to Christ, crowds were dumbfounded to see Christians joyfully going to their deaths with smiles on their faces and rejoicing on their lips. During early persecutions certain bishops were forced to instruct their people not to deliberately bring about their own martyrdom, such was the enthusiasm for rushing to be with Christ. This was because Christians understood that death is the means to glory, and we must see that it remains so.

The martyrs have shed their blood for the sake of their faith, but also for the sake of both purity and dogma. The majority of recorded Christian martyrdom has certainly been for faith in Christ, but a witness to the spirit of our modern age is the death of those who renounced impurity and materialism: we are so encumbered by sin that it is difficult for us to fully grasp how many early Christians saw death as favourable to impurity. A number of women saints in particular considered defilement of their bodies (which was often a part of the punishment handed down to them for being Christian) as worse than death and shed their blood to maintain virtue. One such example was Saint Veronica. When Muslim soldiers stormed her monastery it was clear that they intended to rape her. She avoided this by pretending that a jar of oil had miraculous properties and could immediately heal any wound. Rubbing the oil on her neck she instructed a soldier to strike a blow with his sword. He did so and cut off her head. In horror the soldiers left and Saint Veronica's actions protected not only her own virtue but also that of the other nuns.

Those martyrs who have died for the sake of dogma have bravely defended the faith that has been handed down to us all. Heretics have attacked the teachings of the Church through out its history and some, such as the Arians, have resorted to terrible violence to achieve their aims. A famous example is Saint Theodorous who was dragged behind a horse until he died as part of the slaughter of hundreds of Christians by Arians in Alexandria.

The martyrs have stood before the mightiest powers on earth, they have been falsely accused by kings and judges, but without raising a sword they have been victorious over them all. In weakness God demonstrates strength, and standing alone before the courts of the earth the martyrs have been comforted by the Holy Spirit because every judgement against Christians for their faith is a judgement against God. In our struggles we must not desire worldly power to enforce our will; we are called to be humble and meek even when the world laughs at our foolishness. Sickness and bereavement can make us feel very weak; it can isolate us and make us feel powerless. But we must find that same consolation in God and trust in His love for us, believing that He works all things for our benefit. Saint John Chrysostom even taught that death is a blessing because it frees us from the sorrows of this world and brings to an end our sinning. That which is the fruit of sin is turned by God into a means of liberation. In the Wisdom of Sirach we also read: *O death, how welcome is your sentence to one who is in need.* But martyrdom is more than finding freedom from the pain of life; it is the means by which heavenly crowns are granted. That which is evil is transfigured, death itself becomes a means to glorify God and the light of faith is able to shine into the darkest and most evil places on earth where men commit their worst possible acts. That which was created by the devil in his hatred for God and man becomes a means to great honour for Christians. Only through Christ's death and resurrection is this possible, for without them martyrdom would be empty sacrifices of no more worth than those offered by the pagans. Illness and old age can often bring sufferings and though it may not appear as heroic or profound as giving away this life in an instant, such experiences are an opportunity to practise the same steadfastness as the martyrs perform. Saint Peter writes:

Do not consider it strange concerning the fiery trial which is to try you, as though some strange thing happened to you, but rejoice to the extent that you partake of Christ's sufferings, that when His glory is revealed, you may also be glad with exceeding joy (1 Peter 4$^{12-13}$).

All of us should adopt this same attitude towards our daily and routine struggles. We must not become deluded and think only of dramatic displays of faith, most Christians in the West have not been martyred in this sense, but we should recognise the ongoing pains and demands of this distorted world as our opportunity to endure for Christ. This may be particularly true when we are bereaved and the consequences of sin and death cause us such severe grief. Thus martyrdom addresses the deep mystery that sits at the heart of human life: how we can rejoice and be joyful when life is full of horrors. It is the very paradox of the cross – the shameful death of criminals that becomes the glory and victory of God – that is the constant reality of Christianity. As Saint Paul says *The wisdom of this world is foolishness to* God (1 Corinthians 3^{19}). Therefore we can only perceive the meaning of our suffering through the eyes of faith; worldly logic will only convince us of our tragedy. Only through the guidance of the Holy Spirit can we know what is seen by children but hidden from the worldly wise.

Martyrdom can help free us from our fear of death which results from us not fully embracing the truth of our faith. When we contemplate martyrdom we begin to free ourselves from the materialistic cravings that blind us and bind us to this world. So long as we are bound in this way then we are vulnerable to all that it can do to us. When we are cut free we are no longer panicked by death since it belongs to this world for which we have no attachment. If we live casually, without sober reflection, then we will be victims to the threat of death since we will lose the clear sighted perception of eternal life. Saint Isaac the Syrian writes:

As long as man is careless and indolent in his life, he will fear the hour of death. As long as he depends on worldly knowledge and lives a carnal life, he will be terrified by death.

The martyrs have no fear of death because of their spirituality. They live in close communion with God; their courage flows from the unwavering faith in His promises. If we live as creatures of this world we reduce ourselves to the state of beasts, and all beasts flinch and run at the prospect of death. But if we live as children of God we can overcome this animalistic desire to preserve our life at all costs. The animals do not have a knowledge of the future life, they cannot conceive of heavenly rewards. Atheism plunges the soul into the same terrible condition as dumb animals in this respect: in the martyrs we recognise the highest levels of human development; they have already died to this world before their bodies have been killed. And so, living to God they enter eternal life even before biological death, and the hands of their persecutors cannot harm them.

Martyrdom brings in to focus the seriousness with which we should live. When we indulge in superficial thinking we lose sight of the authentic Christian life that we are called to lead. Earlier we mentioned the ascetic aspect of Christianity, but in being prepared for death we must live a crucified life. Taking up our cross as Christ instructed us will help prepare us for the laying down of our lives whether with or without the shedding of our blood. For the martyrs it mattered not whether they lived because all fear had been taken from them. We can be spiritually paralysed by fear, it prevents us from achieving what might be perceived as risky or even dangerous and it is a consequence of a lack of trust in God.

The death of a martyr is the exact opposite of that of someone who dies unrepentant in their sins: this should be our real fear, not death. The heroic and noble death of a martyr leads to glory, while the fearful death of a sinner is full of shame. Injustice or anything that seems unfair will be made right; we must not allow our longing for things to be the way we want them in this world to prevent us from finding relief from our burdens.

There is an additional effect that comes from contemplating martyrdom and that is the psychological comfort it can bring. When we are troubled by the circumstances of our lives we can find peace of mind if we remember the holy men and women so filled with God's Grace that torture and death could not diminish their joy. Seeing the insignificance of most of our daily trials in comparison to their sufferings should give us a true perspective and encourage us to be more courageous in life. Thinking of ourselves as unimportant and the physical discomforts we briefly have to bare should enable us to practise patience.

If it was our purpose to live eternally in this life then biological death would be a tragedy and certainly something to be avoided. There are some people who live with a bizarre fantasy about their own sense of immortality, never engaging with the inevitability of their death. But our purpose is to pass through the threshold of death to a greater reality. If we see death as part of this process then it is not something to be feared or avoided. If the evils of this world should demand our physical life then they only send us more quickly to glory. If we have lost someone we love we should not want to bring them back and rob them of their reward, since Christ has opened Paradise for us. The martyrs demonstrate the peace that can be ours if we share their faith. As Saint John Chrysostom says:

Let none fear death, for the death of the Saviour has set us free.

Christ is risen and the demons have fallen.

Christ is risen and the angels rejoice.

Killing

Death reminds us that we are not masters of ourselves or our lives. We do not set the limits by which our span is measured; we cannot add a single day to the life God has granted us. Life is a gift from God but it remains His to do with as He wills. Death raises many questions but also provides a true perspective on how we are to live. In this chapter we shall consider how Christian belief provides us with a framework with which we can reflect on the matter of taking another human life in the form of euthanasia, suicide, abortion, and capital punishment.

Death serves to focus our thinking on these issues precisely because we are aware that all our lives will come to an end: we are not deciding to end something that would otherwise have gone on uninterrupted. In the Old Testament there are laws which permit the taking of life; in Genesis Chapter 9 for example it says *Whoever sheds the blood of man by man shall his blood be shed* and in Exodus Chapter 21 we read *Whoever strikes a man a mortal blow must be put to death*. There are a number of crimes which the Law of Moses considers worthy of death such as adultery and blasphemy and those who favour the use of capital punishment often point to these as evidence that God supports their position.

To find the Orthodox view on this is not a simple matter since the issue has really only been one of contention for the last hundred years. Prior to this there was little discussion over the morality of the state punishing certain crimes with the death penalty and Orthodox theologians were as quiet on the subject as everyone else before the twentieth century. We should therefore try to take an even-handed approach and consider the arguments from both sides of the debate.

Those who argue for the death penalty often point to the sense of natural justice that it fulfils, claiming that someone who takes a life has lost the right to their own. This rests on the idea that life is sacred and that the only suitable punishment for those who take it from another must forfeit their own. Supporters claim that it provides a suitable deterrent for certain crimes and that it ensures a level of protection for the weaker members of society as well as ridding wider society of those people who threaten the good order that civilised life requires.

Opponents point to the states in the U.S.A. that use the death penalty and identify that they have the highest rates of murder and other serious crime which, though it may be a complicated matter involving many issues, undermines the idea of it being a deterrent. They also point to the sacredness of life but use it as an argument against the state's right to kill because, they say, only God has such authority. They also point out that flawed justice systems inevitably make mistakes and can never bring back someone wrongly executed for a crime. It is also a fact that in the U.S.A. the vast majority of those who are executed are black and from underprivileged backgrounds.

In the context of our reflection on death we should try to view the matter more theologically. All of us are sinners and it is Satan's desire that we die unrepentant. If we execute a man before he has had the opportunity to repent then certainly Satan rejoices. I have worked in prisons with men who have committed terrible and even evil crimes, and I have no doubt that they deserve to be punished. But amongst them I met men who outwardly gave the impression that they were genuinely facing up to their crimes and wanted to repent. It is possible, of course, as anyone who has worked in prisons will know only too well, that these men were attempting to present something of a reforming if not reformed character in the hope of gaining an earlier release. But if we accept that even one of them was genuine (and I think there were more than that) then we must accept that the desire to repent was prompted by the Holy Spirit. If God chooses to move the heart of a man to repentance, we must ask ourselves whether it can be right to remove anyone's opportunity for this to happen to them. And further we must acknowledge that if God is leading someone to repentance then there must be a possibility of their salvation since God would have no reason to initiate repentance if there were no hope for them. Can we ever say that anyone is beyond hope? Is there any man so corrupted that they are incapable of rehabilitation of transformation? When we contemplate the horror that results from certain actions our efforts should surely be focussed on leading the perpetrator to enter into that same realisation of horror. This is the nature of repentance for all of us, we can only change when we are able to see our true sinful nature in all its horror.

The state does not only take the lives of criminals, medical technology is making the issue of euthanasia a question more people are wrestling with as increasing numbers of people face a prolonged old age which often ends in a death that is extended by drugs and medical equipment. The idea that their death will be dragged out over an unnaturally extended period of time concerns many people and there is evidence of growing support in the western world for state sanctioned euthanasia where death is particularly painful or undignified. Of course, it is ironic that liberal opponents to the death penalty who call lethal injections cruel and inhuman are often the loudest supporters of giving other people the option of taking those drugs.

In many hospitals there are people lying in beds at this very moment whose physical life is being sustained by medical intervention beyond anything that could be termed natural. Amongst some doctors there is a sense that the death of a patient is always a defeat, and I have witnessed families, while longing for a relative to be allowed to die have faced the emotional roller-coaster of resuscitation on a number of occasions. The fact is, it is right to allow people to die when intervention will not restore the person to anything recognisably being their former self. However, this is a different issue to the intervention intended to bring about the death of a patient.

The desire for a comfortable and pain free life is something we are encouraged to seek in the affluent northern hemisphere. Happiness if often equated with a long life and a peaceful, comfortable death. And while few of us would long for a drawn out death resulting from a painful disease, we must at the same time accept the providence of God. The difficult times in our lives can often prove those periods when we make most spiritual advancement. The humbling effect of being dependant on others, the love and patience it may evoke from carers, the reliance on God it may draw out from us may all contribute to the process of our transfiguration: unlike the doctors who may see defeat in the wasting body of a dying man, we may be shown the suffering of the cross and the dignity of God that shines through weakness.

But we must avoid legalism. To accept that in one situation a particular course of action is appropriate is not to set a precedent for all future cases. We are not lawyers but receivers of Grace. It is possible to imagine a situation where the most loving and compassionate act is to administer a substantial dose of morphine that will subdue pain but also end someone's life. This is not an acceptance of the principles of euthanasia only a recognition that in every unknown situation we should be open to God's will.

When discussing the taking of life we should also consider the issue of suicide. Everything that God does is life affirming, the Holy Spirit is the Giver of life. To deliberately take one's own life contravenes this basic impulse, it is a rejection of the gift of life and a failure in the stewardship with which we are entrusted. While the Church will not provide a funeral service to one who has committed suicide we do recognise that it is an act of despair and worthy of compassion. This may seem a contradiction to some, but as we shall see later, the funeral service has a specific function and nature which suicide acts against. To die in the act of taking a life is a grave and perilous thing to do, it denies the individual the opportunity to repent of the very sin they are performing. The Church offers prayers for those who deliberately kill themselves and even in these situations does not lose hope, nevertheless none of us should wish to face Almighty God having deliberately ended a precious life. For life is not ours to do with as we wish, it continues to be the possession of God; He sustains life moment by moment: it is not something he has given to us and then walked away from.

Although there are some pitfalls with modern psychology one of its achievements is the recognition of depression as an illness. Sufferers carry an invisible cross that at times can feel unbearable. When these episodes occur it is vital that we seek the healing of God through the sacraments. We must seek out other Christians and find human comfort where it is offered. Satan wants us isolated and vulnerable and we must protect ourselves against the harm he would do us. The Church recognises with compassion the confusion and diminished capacity to reason that some mental illnesses cause, and none of us should fall into judgement of another, but let none of us fail to recognise the evil that results in suicide.

Perhaps the form of killing that evokes the most emotive response is that of abortion. Many people become angry in defence of the unborn because of the issue of vulnerability. In the West there have been times when the Church has identified a difference between the early stages of pregnancy before the baby was recognised as "quickening", that is becoming truly a live person. Amongst liberal thinkers in the Anglican Church there remain many who consider the well-being of the mother as taking precedence over the life of the child although amongst most Anglicans and certainly Roman Catholics there is an agreed opposition to abortion except where the mother's life is at risk should the pregnancy be allowed to continue. The Orthodox position has always been very clearly against abortion. The Didach (written in the first century) puts it bluntly: *You shall not slay the child by abortion*. This is echoed by many of the early Church Fathers, Tertullian writes *The life of the womb may not be destroyed* because he says *life begins with conception; because we contend that the soul begins at conception.* His teaching is based on the understanding of the union of soul and body, that since we are made up of both the spiritual and physical natures of our being both begin their existence at the same time.

Saint Basil the Great warns that *The woman who purposely destroys her unborn child is guilty of murder*. This is in agreement with the Sixth Ecumenical Council which established that those who provide drugs for the purpose of abortion are to be *subject to the same penalty as murderers*. We find this position repeated time and again in the writings of Origen, Saint Clement of Alexandria, Saint John Chrysostom, Saint Ephraim the Syrian and many more. Modern ethicists have muddied the water with talk of viability (ability to live outside the womb) when in reality the issue is simply one of whether it is permissible to take the life of a human being before he or she is born. Issues raised by technology are a side-show for the real moral question of the deliberate taking of human life. Some argue on the basis of quality of life, that the issue of a motherless child or a family living with the financial burden of many children should be given consideration when deciding on whether to permit abortion. But as Christians we must accept that a human being who has the potential to grow spiritually in the knowledge of God should not be denied that possibility on the grounds of poverty or inconvenience to others. Abortion turns the blessing of God into a curse, and despite the sensitivity of modern ears, let us not cease to call it murder.

The taking of an individual life is one thing, but war raises the possibility of many and even countless deaths. There are pacifists who argue that whether we take a human life on the battlefield or do it in the street, it amounts to the same thing. But the issue is complicated and certainly when we look through history we see that Orthodox Christians have participated in war believing themselves to be doing God's will. Of course all sides in war like to claim God is their ally, but we must consider whether war is ever justifiable.

The Just War Theory is often quoted by western Christians as a basis for deciding which wars are acceptable to God, but Orthodox tradition has not followed this line of thinking. There have been cases where the Church has called the faithful to defend the weak and even the state when it has been closely allied to Christianity. But the Orthodox refused to participate in the Roman crusades (in fact some Orthodox cities suffered more brutality at the hands of Roman Catholic crusaders than they did under invading Muslims) and have attempted to maintain strong theological perspectives over the issue of war. This is because many early Orthodox writers (for example Tatianus and Athenagoras) denounced any Christian involvement in war but at the same time wrote with understanding for those Orthodox who found them selves fighting in battle.

The earliest Christians certainly maintained a strong opposition to any violence and martyrdom was believed to be favourable to fighting. But when the empire professed itself to be Christian many wondered if protecting the borders of Christendom was not service to God's will. While Christ did not fight He is not recorded as condemning any of the soldiers He encountered in a world where brutal conflict was commonplace. In fact early Christians resisted military service on the grounds that soldiers were required to swear oaths to Caesar which was contrary to their faith rather than as a result of any theological objection to war. This ambiguity continues to exist, the Church does not condemn anyone who serves in the military (on the contrary our priests bless troops) but at the same time does not proclaim war as holy (as in lesser jihad). Soldiers returning from war are refused

183

Holy Communion for a number of years in order that they may first recover from their experiences, but they are not rejected as murderers. The taking of life in any situation is to be avoided whenever possible but in order to defend the lives and freedoms of the weak it is sometimes considered acceptable. While the moral choices we make as individuals may free us from the option to kill, international and even global politics may result in the need for military forces to be deployed to defend groups from genocide or oppression. Orthodoxy recognises that governments cannot stand back and allow terrible persecution to take place. Sadly, we are imperfect people, and governments do not always deploy our forces in such noble circumstances.

Taking a human life is the most serious of actions anyone dare perform, it denies a person the opportunity of fulfilling their purpose and is an act over which the demons rejoice. Every person is a child of God but when someone uses their freedom to inflict terrible harm on others then Christians must rightly protect the weak.

Grief and Bereavement

In grief so many of us follow like the women of Jerusalem to Golgotha. Not like Saint Peter who followed from afar, we hold and weep over our dead or dying. But we are called to see that the cross is not simply an instrument of torture and death but a means to our redemption. We cannot remain fixed at the point of the cross, we must move beyond it to what follows. And so we must place the cross at the centre of our ordinary lives in order that it may become the prism through which we see life and the world. The cross is suffering, there is no secret route to avoid it like Buddhism would have us imagine. To love is to make one self vulnerable; if we are to truly love then we must accept that it will bring suffering. The open arms of crucifixion symbolise an open gesture of acceptance and willingness to be vulnerable. We must not try to live our lives closed and protected: this is a rejection of love. Therefore we must see grief as the sting of love when the one we love dies. To be Christian is to be crucified and bereavement is a cross most of us must bare at some point in our lives. It isn't a Christian duty to believe so much in eternal life that we are untouched by someone's death; that would be a grotesque distortion of what it means to be a human being. Christ grieved over His friend Lazarus even before He was about to raise him from the dead. The reality of bereavement cannot and should not be brushed aside but neither must we allow it to overwhelm us.

Since we are created in God's image we are in the image of the Holy Trinity. This tells us that our fulfilment and our purpose is to be realised in our relationships: both to God and to one another. The perfect unity and love of God are shared within God as Three Persons; we are not created in the image of One Who is isolated and alone. Therefore the death of a loved one is not simply an emotional or psychological loss; the death of someone we love can wound us emotionally, psychologically and spiritually. Very often we find excellent advice about the first two types of injury, but very little addresses the spiritual nature of bereavement. In this chapter we will attempt to consider all of these aspects of grief by recognising them as parts of a single whole. Bereavement leaves no part of us unhurt and it is important that we allow ourselves to feel that pain.

As with all spiritual wounds bereavement requires healing. Through out this book we have repeatedly reminded ourselves that the Church is the source of God's care like a spiritual hospital. When we are in grief we need to give time to prayer and receive Holy Communion. We need to enter worship and allow ourselves to be in God's presence but participation in the Eucharist is particularly important because through our association with Christ's eternal life we participate in a profound way with the Kingdom of God within which our loved ones dwell. The Eucharist brings us closer to the dead who are with God and it can be a great source of comfort as well as direct healing. The soul needs time to heal like any other part of us, and we must seek the proper medicine. The support of other Christians is vital; we need their prayer and faith. We must avoid allowing ourselves to become isolated so that our loss becomes ours alone. Within the body of the Church we can discover the shared grief that is experienced by those who love: Saint Paul identifies human comfort when we are *weeping with those who weep* (Romans 12[15]). And as we shall see when we look at the funeral service in the next chapter, we have real things that we can do for the benefit of those who have died. Our link with them is not destroyed and we are not made helpless by grief: it does not wipe away the impact of our love for those who have died. The tomb does not possess us when we die, and neither should we imagine the souls of the dead trapped with their bodies in the grave. Our psychological approach to bereavement affects us emotionally and spiritually, and similarly our faith will have an enormous impact on our mind. We benefit enormously from staying focussed on the reality of eternal life, and on all that Christ achieved in His resurrection. So often depression and unresolved grief can result when our thinking is confused or uncertain. Clear thinking can help us hold firm to God and enable us to receive His healing. Too often sentimental ideas or even heretical beliefs can lead people astray and raise unnecessary fears. It is important that we understand the Church's teaching about death and what happens to us after it so that we safeguard our emotions from demonic attempts to mix uncertainty into our grief.

There are countless examples in the Bible of people in grief. The reality of human life is portrayed in all its pain through the stories of humanity's encounters with God. King David grieved over his sons Amnon and Absalom; Abraham mourned and wept over his wife Sarah; Joseph fell across his dead father Jacob and kissed him in grief; Mary Magdalene wept as she approached Christ's tomb, and even Jesus was moved to tears over the death of Lazarus. Faith in the resurrection does not make us immune to loss and we must not subject ourselves to artificial expectations about how we try to cope with bereavement. Many men are especially bound by social convention when it comes to expressing grief: mothers should be mindful about how they bring up their boys and the kinds of norms they communicate about manhood and strength. If we suppress our grief it can fester like any wound and can lead to far greater injury at a later date. It can be frightening to have to face our loss and there are many people who simply run away from painful feelings. We must not use our faith as a smokescreen for such denial; the wounds of grief must be given the appropriate care needed by any wound.

When someone dies there are often a range of reactions and emotions that people feel. It is true that when we consider a large number of cases certain patterns can be identified in how people respond, but we must not imagine there is a set routine or time-scale that the bereaved must follow. Each of us enters grief with a different story, a different relationship with the one who has died, we each bring to our loss different strengths and needs and the circumstances of our lives will vary greatly. Bereavement for some will come at the end of a long marriage that has been filled with joy, others will lose spouses feeling that issues have been left unresolved. Some will lose children before they have had a chance to know anything of life; the situations are as individual as the people who have died. But grief does bring certain identifiable features that are common to many people as well as symptoms that may be exhibited by fewer people.

Grief in its more acute form can render an individual numb or left in a state of shock. It can take away people's ability to think clearly or remember the most basic things (it is often a good idea to avoid making important decisions immediately after someone's death). But more commonly the bereaved will find they cannot sleep, that their moods may change without obvious reason and grief often brings feelings of guilt or even shame (particularly common when it is a young child who has died). Many people who lose a loved one will experience a sense of anger whether directed at the dead person for leaving, at medical staff for not doing more, or at God for allowing such things to happen. A Methodist minister friend described to me an occasion when, during a visit to arrange a funeral, the widow attacked him with the family Christmas tree: he was the tangible sign of a God she blamed for her loss. In short, our reactions can be irrational and unpredictable, we may feel stuck in a particular emotion for a long time or we may feel ourselves jumping from one to another in quick succession. The trauma of bereavement can be accompanied by a sudden change in lifestyle if the dead person was someone we were dependent on for practical assistance or can result in sudden financial difficulties if they earned the main income for the family. And of course, no matter how common many of these problems are, when it happens to us it can feel like we are the only person in the world who knows what it's like.

I remember serving a funeral many years ago with a funeral director who liked to chat and make jokes with people. He was good at his job, he went to great lengths to provide any service families would request, but he often exhibited little empathy towards what the grieving family was experiencing emotionally. As we stood at the entrance to the graveyard waiting for the hearse to arrive, he made his usual jokes. As we laughed I looked up to see the family had arrived unexpectedly only to catch us chuckling merrily before the internment of the coffin. Looking into the eyes of the bereaved I understood the distance between their reality and ours, we were like two impostors who must have looked to them like we were just going through the motions. The shame I felt in that moment brings into sharp focus the isolation grief can force onto someone. While the world around them continues to pursue the same superficial concerns the bereaved know a stark new vividness to existence, all pretence has been stripped from them as they see the reality of our mortality.

Paradoxically it is the case that some people find it difficult to allow themselves to move on from their grief because to do so feels like a betrayal of the one who has died. Some of us sometimes fear losing the intensity of memory that grief seems to bring and to recover may appear like another kind of letting go. In fact healing does not diminish the person's importance to us: most people discover that they are able to once again feel joy in their memories of the dead once the pain has subsided.

It is crucial for the bereaved to be given the freedom to grieve at their own pace and in their own way. No one should be allowed to dictate your grieving to you, whether in terms of how or for how long. They may feel they have a sense of your psychological make-up but they do not know your spiritual reality. Eventually we have to gain perspective on our loss and this requires the healing process to be allowed to move forward. What may initially bring horror and abandonment can lead to growth and renewed powers: many bereaved people go on to discover new emotional wells which they did not imagine they had, or else they may learn deeper patterns of prayer as they struggle to cope with their pain. The heightened perception of life and death can intensify people's sensitivity to God and spiritual truths; it is far more than just a journey through the emotions.

Ecclesiastes reminds us that there is a *time to weep*: the death of someone we love is one of those times. It is not a sign of someone having little faith when they shed tears; Christ shed tears more than once in His love for others. Weeping is a healthy and natural response to grief, it is biologically linked to our inner state. To weep can often help us to recognise our dependency on God; it can open our eyes to our inability to always be strong and in control of life. Grief can help us develop greater humility but also patience. As we pass through the time of grief we can often long for change to come

192

more quickly. Our longing for healing helps us to rely on God's mercy; we can learn to wait on the wisdom of God's timing and not the schedule we want life to follow.

Grief must ultimately teach us to trust in God. Only when we accept that our loved one is in the hands of God can we gain peace. Similarly we may become aware of how badly we have behaved towards someone while they were alive. Grief can prompt us to seek God's forgiveness but also make us aware of our own death and the coming judgement.

Having recognised the human need to grieve, we should also acknowledge that since we are not destined to remain here on earth but join our loved ones in eternity we must not allow grief to overcome us. Saint Basil writes:

Those who have been united during the course of this present life and later are separated by death resemble travellers journeying on a single road. Having become used to travelling together, they have been joined closely on account of their companionship. But when they reach the point where they must part, and each one is obliged to follow his own way, they are not restrained by the companionship they enjoyed together. They part and each goes his own way. So is the case now; you travel along with your beloved relative – the spouse; the mother; the child- but the time has come to part.

A certain robustness is required in facing death this way. Our mind must be set on the promise that our loved one is cherished by God, and we must learn to live without their physical and psychological support. We must throw ourselves onto God who must be our true support, only God can provide the unending hope that our soul requires. We must recognise that God loves our dead and us far more than we love each other. Perhaps it grieves us not to be able to see the face that looks so beautiful to us, or share in the soul which is tender. But that soul is now celebrating in the heavenly feast: let this truth fill our hearts. God knows all and everything falls within His plan for us. What may appear like a terrible tragedy from our earthly perspective will come to have a greater meaning when God reveals all to us. And so for now we must have faith that we are loved and what appears chaotic according to our limited perception will be revealed as working to God's plan for us. As the words of Ecclesiastes remind us:

To everything there is a season, a time for every purpose under heaven: a time to weep and a time to laugh; a time to mourn and a time to dance.

At the beginning of this chapter we observed that it is love that makes us grieve, but we should also recognise that it is love that gives meaning to death and makes our grief bearable. Christ's love infuses our grief with hope. As we are being transformed through this process of theosis so our emotions are transfigured through the power of the resurrection. The Holy Spirit does not tamper with the edges of our soul; He illuminates the deepest and darkest places of our existence. When grief cuts to the very core of who we are, it is here that God meets us and transforms us. As difficult as it may sound when grief is new, God can change the bitterness of grief to sweetness through our faith in His gift of eternal life.

When we read the Psalms it quickly becomes clear that at no point does God condemn our grief but understands it as part of the consequence of the reality of death. To conclude this chapter we should remember that this world is not as God intended it but as we made it. This life is full of pain and sorrow, and despite the image of life presented in the movies, most people struggle with their lot. We are called then to adopt an understanding of our time on earth as a brief preparation for eternity. Both the pleasures and the pains of this world will pass and we must learn to recognise the transient nature of both. Death of our loved ones creates a brief separation which we must endure, but only for a while. Yes, we must be honest and express the grief we feel, but let our hearts be like that of the Prophet Job who rejoiced in God even in the face of desolation.

The Funeral

The first thing we must acknowledge when talking about funerals is that the service for a Christian is a very different occasion to that of an atheist. The funeral emphasises the belief in eternal life, without which the service could only be empty words and pointless ceremony. Christian funerals emphasise the dignity and worth of the individual and they involve us in the continuing life of the deceased person through prayer. The bond between the living and the dead is palpable at an Orthodox funeral, so that as well as sorrow there is a sober joy rooted in faith in Christ's resurrection. In this penultimate chapter we will consider the purpose and practices of Orthodox funerals and also reflect on the issue of cremation.

First we should recall that Christianity identifies a person as both soul and body; therefore what is done with the body is important. Treating the body with respect also demonstrates to the living the correct attitude to our physical being while alive since it reminds us of its value and place within our salvation. The earth of the grave will be the body's bed only until the Day of Resurrection when it will be reunited with the soul for all eternity. The body was given its dignity when God first breathed life into it and when man defaced it God again gave it back its worth through the incarnation. Finally God raised our human form into Himself when Christ ascended into Heaven and so we too do God's will when we honour the body, both in life and in death. We wrap the dead body in a shroud which represents the dress of incorruption which we believe the person will receive. We pour oil and myrrh on the body just as it was anointed at baptism.

If death is known to be imminent then it is the custom for the dying person to receive the sacramental support of a priest. Making confession and receiving communion is the best way to prepare ourselves in the final period before we die, and since none of us knows when our hour of death is going to be it is advisable to receive the sacraments as a regular part of our ordinary lives.

Immediately after death the priest will sing the Trisagion prayers and this is often done on the night before the funeral service as well: in Greece many families choose to pay their respects to the body of the deceased during these prayers. The forty day period of prayers following someone's death is often accompanied by a period of formal mourning, and many Orthodox will avoid social events during this period. It is not unknown for some widows or widowers to extend this observance beyond the forty days and in Greece it is a familiar sight to see an elderly woman who has chosen to wear black for the rest of her life. Recent criticisms in the United Kingdom of Queen

Victoria attribute her remaining in black (even though she was not Orthodox) to unresolved grief but this simply fails to understand the cultural practices of other countries. It is interesting to note how common it is amongst non-believers in the U.K. to request that those attending a funeral should dress in happy, colourful clothing. This refusal of the normal trappings of grief quickly feels out of place when the congregation is confronted with the coffin sitting silently in the centre of the church: suddenly denial of what has happened can feel ridiculous.

The funeral expresses the belief that the soul has been unconditionally surrendered to God. We sing *I am the lost sheep; call me again O Saviour* and *do Thou lead me back to Thy likeness.* The funeral acknowledges that death has shown those who live that they are utterly dependent on God no matter how strong the illusion is that we are in control. In death we see the truth; it is something we race towards despite often distracting ourselves with false comforts. But in life as in death our only hope is God and at the funeral service we see our wealth, status, health and everything which feeds our pride as no more than vanity. We see the dead lying in church stripped of any earthly claims, only the condition of the soul now counts before God, that is the virtues and vices with which they are dressed. As Saint Basil writes:

Look carefully upon the grave and, if you can, distinguish who is the servant and who is the master, who is the poor and who is the rich. Separate, if you can, the prisoner from the king, the strong from the weak, the beautiful from the ugly.

It is in this context that our prayers are offered, we surround our loved ones with petitions to God for their salvation, for now their lips are silent and it is left to us to join the angels in intercession. We ask God for the remission of the deceased person's sins, not in an attempt to change God's mind, but to express our love for them as parts or members of the one Body. Death has not separated them from the Body of Christ; we continue to have a duty to pray for one another.

Towards the end of the funeral service the congregation gathers to kiss either the veiled head of the dead or else an icon placed in their hands. It is a moving acknowledgement of the body which was united to the soul in life but also a sign that it is this same body now corrupted which will rise in glory. The body is the vessel or temple into which God breathed life, to honour it with something so intimate as a kiss removes any possibility of seeing the body as now alien or to be feared. Just as we kiss icons, altars and Gospel books so we now kiss the departed as a sign that in death they are still worthy of honour, a practice that comes from the kissing of Christian martyrs before their deaths which was incorporated into the funeral service around the fourth or fifth century. The kiss also marks the union between the Church on earth and in Heaven, an expression of human love in Christ that is not destroyed by death.

After forty days are over commemoration services are held and again after six months and then annually. The priest will also commemorate the dead as he mixes the bread into the wine at the Divine Liturgy; it is important that people approach their priest and ask for this to be done. The Eucharist unites us to the resurrection of Christ and the Church teaches that commemoration of the dead in this way is the most powerful of prayers we can offer for them. Praying in this way makes us co-workers with God Who already knows everything that we need but permits us to participate in His blessing of us.

Clearly the funeral service both does something and expresses belief: it is an action of love which also proclaims faith in resurrection. The practice of cremation also expresses a belief but one that is entirely opposed to Christianity. The burning of the body is a denial of its worth. Hindus and Buddhists cremate the body of the dead to deliberately proclaim that its value is passed; it is a shell which has been cast off so that the soul may move on to another. The destruction of the body in this way insists that it is only the soul that matters. Through out history the practice has been forbidden for Orthodox but in the West today there are an increasing number of people who have lost touch with the Christian faith. Even amongst some liberal theologians of the Anglican tradition there are some who argue that Christ's resurrection was only of a spiritual nature and did not involve His body. It is a denial that our whole person has been called to salvation and is a product of neo-pagan philosophies which have no place in the Christian faith. We bury the body facing east in the belief that they will rise to be judged by Christ on the final day, the candles we light proclaim that they have passed from darkness to Christ's light.

While it is sometimes necessary to cremate the body, for example if the remains pose a threat to the living, in normal circumstances an Orthodox funeral service will not be permitted if someone has elected to be cremated. This is because the denial of resurrection simply cannot be accepted, it is abhorrent to us. In Britain today increasing numbers of people seek cremation because the plain council buildings demand no response or pose no difficult questions. Most crematoriums are forbidden to display any Christian imagery for fear of offending non-Christians and so the twenty minutes of what often amounts to nothing more than a few kind words is over and the next family is waiting to be shown in. It is a production line that wipes away any sign that a life was lived and the family is later presented with a jar of grit and ash.

For the British it began in 1822 when the drunken friends of the poet Shelly burned his body on an Italian beach after he had drowned. Stories of the event drifted back to England and acquired an undeserved romance. As huge municipal cemeteries became places of grave robbing and disease a doctor named Henry Thomson brought back to England ideas from Italy about burning bodies. He even argued that the ashes could be used as fertilizer but his main claim was that it was a suitable way of controlling disease. Debate raged about the issue until 1882 when Thomas Hanham built his own oven and burned the body of his wife. After a number of court cases and various protests where people secretly had bodies cremated, the argument for cremation gathered pace until the 1890s when a number were built in England. The practice spread across Britain: Pontypridd has the dubious honour of being the first place in Wales to witness the cremation of a body. Despite papal threats of excommunication in earlier years, Roman Catholics were granted official permission to have cremation in 1963.

As stated earlier, if you have a family member who has been cremated you must not become unduly upset, but trust that God is able to gather and restore the body regardless of its condition. But as Christians we must reject the practice since it represents a rejection of hope and introduces a sense of man's control over these matters. When we bury our dead we do so with expectant hearts, God's earth receives the body and holds it until time is no more. From the earth we were created and to the earth we return, our bodies planted like seeds waiting for God to call them forth. These bodies receive Christ, they are the temple of the Holy Spirit, let us treat them as such and not burn and grind them to dust like those who see death as the end. We have certainty of eternal life, and our bodies are the gift of God in which we work to receive salvation.

The funeral service repeatedly reminds us of God's infinite mercy and goodness towards man. This is why we have hope, because in God there is always hope. The funeral service is a great comfort to us because through it we see that no matter how sinful we or our departed loved ones are, nothing can rob us of this hope. The funeral service prompts us to repent as we lay before God Who has trampled down death by death, the soul of the departed seeking entry into Paradise. It is a moment to reflect on how each of us travels our journey in the loving hands of God; through life and into death we place ourselves entirely in His care. But for Christians there must be recognition that death marks the departure from toil and sorrows to a place where death and suffering is no more. This earth offers no joy that is not tinged with sorrow, but the funeral service calls us to have hearts that are sorrowful but tinged with rejoicing.

Emotionally we may be suffering at the temporary separation that death brings, but our hearts cling to the joy of Christ's promises.

During the funeral service the choir and people sing *Remember me Lord, when You come into Your Kingdom.* In the words of the penitent thief all present acknowledge that like one justly dying in punishment for his sins none of us has a defence against the consequences of our sins. None of us is deserving of any good thing, and yet we cry out to God's mercy. The funeral reminds us of the justice of the all-wise God and denies us any false claim of anger towards Him or even a sense of injustice in the face of death. It is a call for us to mourn our sins not just for the departed, since each of us singing at the funeral will have the same words sung for us.

The funeral service ends with a farewell to the departed. It comes from one living being to another, a final acknowledgement that families and friends will see each other again. It is a painful, moving and beautiful moment that is full of human grief and theological assurance. Though we may not hear one another's voices for a short time, the prayers we offer continue to unite us, as the world perceives only an end, in faith we see a new beginning.

Living With The Knowledge Of Death

Awareness of our death calls us to live in readiness, choosing in everything we do to incline ourselves towards or away from God. In every minor activity, every apparently insignificant thought and feeling we either give ourselves to God or deny His authority over us. If we seek to act in obedience then we find freedom, but clinging to our own will we only enslave ourselves to the emotional and psychological turbulence that swirls within us.

We are each going to die and this time between then and now is our opportunity to change. When we come to stand before God it will be this time that counts for or against us. Our soul will be shaped by the things we have chased or craved, by the goals we have set ourselves and by the way we have treated other people.

Remembering the journey to Golgotha the Christian is called to move out from the crowd that follows Christ at a distance. All safe distance must be removed so that we may reach and embrace the One Who labours beneath His cross. We are called to see this same wounded figure in one another, and journey together sharing the weight of the cross we have been given. The purpose of our life is to be transfigured by God so that even when death brings our material life to an end the soul will live on in eternal union with its Creator. For many it has only been through the willingness to suffer death for the sake of God that this union has been possible.

Our lives are of utmost importance and must not be squandered in triviality. Saint Isaac warns us that *This life has been given to you for repentance, do not waste it in vain pursuits.* Death must always be before our eyes as a solemn focus of where we are headed. But as Saint John Chrysostom writes:

The man who wants to be reminded constantly of death and of God's Judgement, and who at the same time gives in to material cares and distractions, is like someone trying at the same time to swim and to clap his hands.

The remembrance of our death is necessary if we are to live correctly. Our minds are so darkened by sin and materialism that we can quickly begin to imagine this world as something of importance and sink into the comforts and pleasures that it offers. It has been said that he who frequently remembers death has already risen from the dead in his soul. Setting our eyes firmly on eternity leads us to overcome the trials and struggles of life because we understand their brevity and accept the care with which God is making us fit for Paradise.

God has given us awareness of our death so that we may live as exiles in this world, living somewhere between fear and hope in expectation of judgement. If we genuinely seek any kind of spiritual life then our remembrance of death must be daily; there are monastics who say they live in perpetual awareness of its coming. Such thoughts protect us from temptation, they guide us along Christ's narrow path, they prompt compassion and mercy for others and most importantly they fill us with a desire to repent. Remembrance of death makes sin taste bitter and prayer the sweetest of joys. It wakes us from the sleep of this world where men only dream that they live and thrusts us into the reality of God's presence where eternal life is discovered. Knowing that we are going to die is a blessing from God which we must receive and cherish for in this gift is the possibility of salvation.

We must learn to embrace the reality of our death and never let its inevitability become a defeat or a tragedy. Death is the path to victory for the Christian; we must not be faithless and join in the world's confusion. Let us not flinch in the face of our mortality; our hearts must not be dead tombs of lifeless stone but places of resurrection. I have been present at the deaths of about a dozen people through my ministry and each time I have been struck by the nobility of the human body. Even when the person has died from a disease that has caused their body to waste away, at death there is the clear sense that though the person has left their body, it maintains a value that is more than the dead remains of a corpse might suggest. It is very different from the remains of an animal, no matter how dear the creature may have been to us, once life has left a dog or cat the body loses all value and there is no shame in allowing the vet to dispose of them. But a human body remains precious; there is still a link between it and the soul and knowing that it will rise again at resurrection makes it worthy of honour.

This is the perspective we must have on our death. Christ came not just to free us from sin but to give new life. That God should create us to be made gods by Grace should fill us with awe but also lead us to acknowledge the worth of our lives. We may not feel very special at times, but it is important that we recognise the drivers of other cars, the shoppers in the supermarket, the neighbour who plays his music too loud, and even ourselves, as creatures brought into being for communion with the One Who is the source of every good thing that exists. Death is not the end of us, and this life is no more than the prelude to eternity. In Paradise we will know and meet again our friends and family once more and be blessed to love them with a capacity unknown in this world. Our love will be made perfect, our joy will be endless, there will be no sin, no sickness, no tears and no death, it will be an existence of eternal spiritual pleasure: no wonder the martyrs were happy to be sent to their reward. Let us set our eyes firmly on the truth of Christ's promises, and with the Church on earth and in Heaven, let us sing:

Christ is risen from the dead,

Trampling down death by death
And on those in the tombs
Bestowing life.

Glossary

Apostasy – when a Christian deliberately chooses to believe false teaching, it literally means *turning away*. As a sin it has devastating effect on the individual but more serious is the right belief of the Church as a whole without which no one could know the truth.

Ascension – forty days after the resurrection Christ ascended into Heaven from the Mount of Olives. Christ's ascension completes the union of humanity with God since Christ was ascended in the flesh.

Asceticism – in his efforts to develop self-discipline and to crucify the flesh the Christian enters a life of prayer, fasting and self-denial. The word comes from the Greek for *athlete* reminding us of Saint Paul's image of the Christian as one who runs a race and must maintain his efforts until the finish line is crossed.

Assumption – the feast of the dormition or falling asleep of the Theotokos.

Blasphemy – words or actions which aimed to offend or debase God, the saints or sacred actions or objects. Blasphemy against the Holy Spirit is cited by Christ as the one unforgivable sin since it denies the saving action of God.

Burial – the internment of the body as a sign of faith in the General Resurrection.

Canonisation – the official recognition by the Church of someone's righteousness and that they are believed to be in a blessed state before God.

Chrismation – when Christians are baptised into the Orthodox Church they receive the Holy Spirit through this sacrament which involves the anointing with oils. It is the sacramental continuation of the laying on of hands that we find in the New Testament.

Communion – refers to the union between man and God and is commonly associated with the state that a person enters through the Eucharist but holiness of life is vital.

Confession – we use this in two ways: first describing the witness to our faith and secondly the sacrament where we tell our sins to God before our priest and receive absolution (forgiveness or release from them).

Corruption – the condition or state of humanity after the fall from Paradise. It represents our sinfulness and mortality and is the cause of suffering.

Cosmos - this can mean both the world and the universe. It is often used when referring to the effect of sin and of the resurrection, both of which changed the cosmos.

Council – from the Book of Acts onwards the Church has always made its decisions regarding doctrine and Church order through gatherings of bishops. To equate authority in the Church with a single bishop was unknown for the first thousand years of the Church's life and continues to be the case in Orthodoxy.

Creation – we can use this term to refer to God's action of bringing the universe into existence or to the cosmos itself.

Deification – the purpose of the Christian life, growing into the likeness of God through His Grace.

Departed – simply refers to the dead.

Devil – see Satan.

Energy – the uncreated Grace that comes from God which unites us to Him. It is distinguished from the essence of God which remains hidden from us (in mystery).

Essence – the mysterious nature of God in Three Persons which is beyond the perception or understanding of humanity.

Eucharist – from the Greek word for *thanksgiving* it refers to the sacrament of Holy Communion when Christians physically and drink the flesh and blood and so receive God's presence and strength.

Flesh – in the New Testament refers to the fallen nature of man and identifies those influences of the fallen world which inhibit spiritual growth and tempt us into sin.

Free Will – man's ability to make moral choices. This choosing extends to the acceptance or rejection of God and is an aspect of what it means to be created in his image.

Glory – the revealed splendour of God.

Gospel – a term which has its roots in the ancient world where the ascension to the throne of a new ruler would be announced. It can be translated as *Good News* and refers to Christ's call to repentance in readiness for the Kingdom of God.

Grace – the uncreated energy of God experienced by Christians mainly through the sacraments. It is a gift from God and cannot be earned but is not bestowed on those who reject God.

Hades – similar to the Hebrew idea of Sheol, it is the Greek word for the place where the dead dwelt before the resurrection of Christ.

Heart – the location of one's spiritual centre where the Grace of God works within us.

Heresy – teaching which is opposed or differs from the doctrines of the Church. It is one of the most harmful and serious of sins.

Holy – from the Greek word *agios* meaning not of this world. *Agios* is where we get words like geologist and geography, and the prefix simply means not.

Hope – the trust in and sense of certainty about God's goodness.

Hypostasis – the union of existence which is applied to the Three Persons of the Holy Trinity and to the human and divine natures of Christ.

Illumination – can be applied to the sacrament of baptism and to the enlightening of a person by the light of God (which occurs at baptism and chrismation).

Judgement – the revealing by God of the true nature of a person's actions in terms of sin or righteousness.

Kingdom of God – in the Old Testament was associated with the rule of God rather than a place. A person enters the Kingdom of God when they are obedient to God's will.

Liturgy – the worship of God in Church services. The Divine Liturgy is the service of the Eucharist.

Man – through out the Bible (and this volume) the word man refers to human beings rather than those who are male. Of all the creatures God made only man was granted to be in the image and likeness of God and so is recognised as the pinnacle of creation.

Martyr – comes from the Greek word for *witness* and is usually used to describe those who give their lives for their faith in Christ.

Messiah – the Hebrew concept of God's chosen one. While many Jews expected an earthly king who would create God's Kingdom on earth Christ revealed a greater and more profound vision of His role which made the Kingdom available to every human heart.

Mind – sometimes used interchangeably with heart, the mind refers to the faculty for reasoning or the inner person.

New Man – the Christian who is transformed by the Holy Spirit and released from slavery to sin. It is used to distinguish from the *old man* which is he who is not united to Christ or changed by the Holy Spirit.

Paradise – used in two ways: first the place where Adam walked with God and second the eternal state of being with God after death.

Pascha – the Hellenised form of the Jewish word Pesach or Phaska, meaning passage or Passover.

Propitiation – the offering of Himself that Christ made through His suffering and death that leads to the reconciliation of man and God. It results in the liberation of man from sin and death.

Rapture – the heretical belief that God will gather up His Church before the time of tribulations preceding the return of Christ at the end of time.

Redemption – through His resurrection Christ has delivered us from death and the claims over us of Satan.

Remission – The forgiveness of our sins and the forgiveness we show others of their sins committed against us.

Repentance – from the Greek word metanoia which means to turn away from sin or to change one's mind. Repentance is an essential action necessary on the part of man to enter Paradise.

Satan – the angel Lucifer who led rebellion in Heaven and was cast out by God. The Greek word fro devil literally means *separator* referring to his desire to separate us from God's love. While retaining free will the devil has become so corrupted by evil that all repentance is impossible for him and at Judgement he will be cast into eternal punishment.

Second Coming – the return of Christ at the end of time as Judge of the living and the dead to establish a new earth and a new Heaven.

Soul – the invisible, spiritual existence of a man untied to his body.

Spirit – non-material being, it has different uses in the Bible: first the Holy Spirit is the Third person of the Holy Trinity; second the immaterial part of a man which breathed into the body at creation and finally it is the term used to describe the nature of angels which do not have physical bodies.

Theotokos – the Mother of God, Saint Mary. The term was agreed at the Council of Ephesus in order to maintain that it was truly God that was conceived in her womb.

Transfiguration – on Mount Tabor the three disciples witnessed the transformation of Christ and beheld His glory. This event is known as the Transfiguration and the word is also applied to the transformation that we experience through the Grace of the Holy Spirit.

Trisagion Prayer – prayers of *Holy God, Holy Mighty, Holy Immortal have mercy on* *us* which are sung three times. It literally means *thrice holy* and indicates the Three Persons of the Holy Trinity.

Vice – a sinful act which becomes a habit.

Virtue – a good or righteous action which is developed into a characteristic or pattern of behaviour.

THE ANCIENT
PATH

FATHER
SPYRIDON BAILEY

The Ancient Path is an examination of how modern culture and ideas have affected Christianity. It challenges Christians to rediscover the faith of the Early Church as preserved in the doctrines and traditions of Orthodoxy. Fr Spyridon takes the teachings of the Church Fathers as his starting point for each chapter and demonstrates how they apply to us in the twenty-first century.

JOURNEY TO MOUNT ATHOS

FATHER SPYRIDON BAILEY

In 2012 Fr Spyridon visited the heart of Orthodox monasticism. He encountered monks and hermits who have devoted themselves to the ancient pursuit of God on the Greek peninsula known as the Holy Mountain. **Journey To Mount Athos** is a glimpse into a world few of us have known and creates a vivid sense of a way of life that remains unaffected by worldly superficiality.